D0684174

The most rewarding and useful aspect of the book is the treatment of preventative and coping methods that might be used to deal with life stressors—a realistic and practical "How To" approach for the practical-minded reader! Concluding remarks serve as a primer on how to live the best life that a person is capable of living.

I am absolutely convinced that the understandable and practical way in which these authors have presented their information will make *Write Your Own Prescription for Stress* mandatory reading for my patients.

—John P. Lanier, M.D., Atlanta, Georgia

Write Your Own

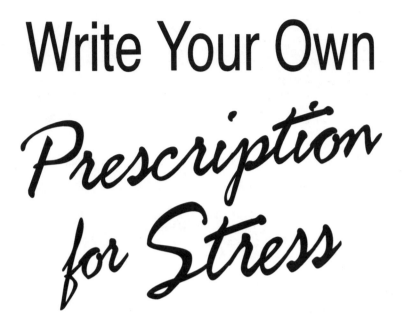

Prescription for Stress

Kenneth B. Matheny, Ph.D., ABPP,
and Christopher J. McCarthy, Ph.D.

New Harbinger Publications, Inc.

Publisher's Note

This publication is designed to provide accurate and authoritative information in regard to the subject matter covered. It is sold with the understanding that the publisher is not engaged in rendering psychological, financial, legal, or other professional services. If expert assistance or counseling is needed, the services of a competent professional should be sought.

Distributed in the U.S.A. by Publishers Group West; in Canada by Raincoast Books; in Great Britain by Airlift Book Company, Ltd.; in South Africa by Real Books, Ltd.; in Australia by Boobook; and in New Zealand by Tandem Press.

Copyright © 2000 by Kenneth B. Matheny and Christopher J. McCarthy
New Harbinger Publications, Inc.
5674 Shattuck Avenue
Oakland, CA 94609

Cover design © 2000 by Lightbourne Images
Edited by Jason Rath
Text design by Tracy Marie Powell

Library of Congress Catalog Card Number: 00-134874
ISBN 1-57224-215-9 Paperback

All Rights Reserved

Printed in the United States of America

New Harbinger Publications' Web site address: www.newharbinger.com

02   01   00

10   9   8   7   6   5   4   3   2   1

First printing

Contents

Part II
Coping with Stress

Acknowledgments

We wish to express our appreciation to the editorial and marketing staffs of New Harbinger Publications for the expert technical assistance offered us throughout the writing of this book. We especially wish to recognize the exceptional editorial assistance of Jason Rath, who seemed to clearly understand from the beginning the purpose of the book and whose gentle and wise guidance helped keep us on track. We often marveled at his uncanny ability to never lose sight of the central threads running throughout the book and to make suggestions for deleting and adding that always seemed eminently appropriate. Deep appreciation is extended as well to Richard J. Riordan, whose clear thinking and keen insights in previously coauthored publications helped to develop many of the ideas expressed herein.

We want also to acknowledge our indebtedness to our students over a combined forty-six years of university teaching. By their challenging questions and shared experiences, they have directed our attention to the critical dimensions of stress and coping as topics of serious inquiry. Special thanks go to Michelle Beard, Naomi Moller, and Blaine Carr, who assisted with researching and reviewing the book.

Most of all, we are deeply grateful to our wives, Mary Matheny and Shelley McCarthy, for their understanding of our need to spend endless hours alone incubating the ideas that eventually took form on these pages. It is to them for their love, patience, and support and to our children—Carolyn, Ron, Janice, and Kurt Matheny and Colleen and Sean McCarthy, who have enriched our lives immeasurably—that we dedicate this book.

Preface: Taming Invisible Tigers

In the primeval forests, our early ancestors were buffeted by the elements and stalked by predators. Their lives were cut short by these life-threatening conditions; in fact, radiocarbon tests of their skeletal remains suggest that most died in their twenties or thirties. Although admittedly luck must have played some role in determining who lived and died, clearly survivors of these dangerous conditions must have been special in some important ways. Perhaps they had sharper surveillance skills. Perhaps they were more vigilant in noticing the lurking figure in the brush or hearing the crackling of twigs from the tiger lying in ambush. Perhaps those who coped best were able to produce adrenaline faster to power their muscles for fight or flight. Whatever the reasons, their superior survival skills allowed them a longer period in which to contribute to the gene pool. Consequently, we have inherited from those survivors a nervous system that beautifully equips us for fight or flight. The process by which the nervous system does this is called the *stress response*.

Today the only real tigers most of us ever see are in zoos. What we now face are *invisible* tigers. Threats to our well-being, once as clear and unambiguous as a charging predator, are now less easily detectable. The invisible tigers are the stressful relationships, stifling work conditions, financial worries, daunting parenting problems, and similar situations we face each day. What's worse, it's often difficult to resolve these more complicated problems. When you go toe-to-toe with a real tiger, success is defined quite plainly: Did you escape or were you the tiger's dinner? Invisible tigers like job-seeking after a layoff, trying to mend a troubled marriage, or helping a son or daughter to do better in school lend themselves to quick solutions only on television programs.

The really bad news is that the stress response that was so valuable in fighting real tigers is of no value at all in fighting the invisible tigers of everyday modern life. In fact, perhaps the biggest battle of all is in fighting the stress response itself! As we'll see in chapters to follow, the frequent elicitation of the stress response may threaten our health, lower our performance, interrupt our relationships with others, and diminish the quality of our lives.

We can't live in this world without encountering conditions that lead to stress and suffering and in many ways, we are well equipped to deal with this reality. Buddhists believe that suffering is the natural condition of the human family. The human brain, a kind of bio-computer, seems programmed to identify and solve problems. Our tendency to forecast the future, to plan and worry about it, may be the reason we aren't living outdoors exposed to the elements along with the rest of the animals. However, fretting about the future serves its purpose only if it is a catalyst to meaningful action. Even so, our natural tendency is to complain about events, worry about their consequences, and yet do nothing about the events themselves. A famous commencement address by *Chicago Tribune* columnist Mary Schmich (1997) (erroneously attributed to Kurt Vonnegut) suggests that worry alone is "about as effective as chewing bubble gum to solve an algebra equation."

However, there is good news. Even though our body's stress response is primitive and inappropriate for adjustment to a modern, technologically advanced society, our minds can help us bridge the gulf between this ancient biology and the requirements of modern living. If we are to tame these invisible tigers, we must build a rich array of stress coping resources. In a study of people aged 100 years or more, Drs. Thomas Perls and Margery Silver (1999) found that one factor these centenarians held in common was their ability to manage stress effectively. They had an average number of stressful experiences, but they were more resilient than others in coping with them.

Everyone knows that it is important to cope effectively with stress. Doing it, however, is quite another matter. Imagine being told every day how critically important it is that *you* travel by rocket to Mars before the year 2010. Impressive-sounding statistics are quoted to you suggesting the disastrous repercussions if you do not. All around you people are discussing the topic, you read about it, and some people seem well on their way to their destination. But you don't have a clue as to how to begin the journey. For most of us, being told that we should master stress is like being told that we should travel to Mars: "Okay, if it's so important," we want to know, "how do we do it?" Much has been written about the subject, some of it groundbreaking. But in our view, most books take one of two approaches to managing stress: (a) a highly specific formula for handling one particular type of stress, such as chronic illness, or (b) a compilation of everything that is known about the subject. Scant attention has been paid to the *process* of coping with stress in a way that is applicable to the experience of most people. In other words, how do you *systematically* get from point A, being stressed, to point B, successful coping?

Psychologists Richard Lazarus and Susan Folkman (1984) were among the first to propose a comprehensive model for coping with stress, and their work spurred tremendous interest among stress researchers. First, they suggested that it is the *meaning* we attach to our experiences that causes stress. Secondly, they proposed that in today's modern, complex world we can deal with stress effectively only by using what we call *coping resources*. Although we cannot always control our environment, we can control our own stressful reactions *if we develop these resources and use them effectively*.

We firmly believe that problems in coping seldom stem from lack of ability or motivation; they more often stem from the lack of a "road map" to guide one's efforts. Although we can't totally escape stressful experiences, we can, with guidance, build a repertoire of effective coping resources. People differ greatly in regard to the completeness of their coping resources. All of us have some coping resources, and some, the expert stress tamers, possess a well-developed collection of them. Some resources have been given to us by birth, and some have been cultivated by loving parents. Others, however, must be carefully crafted by each of us. Regardless of what resources we have, it's important to know when and how to use them. In the following chapters, we'll help you identify an array of the most critical resources for coping. We will also help you to appreciate the value of these resources, and offer strategies and tactics for acquiring them.

This book is divided into two major sections. The first part is devoted to helping you understand what stress is. Chapter 1 provides an overview of the nature of stress, and chapter 2 provides a framework for understanding how the stress response is triggered. Chapter 3 details some of the ways that modern living can contribute to stress. Then, in chapter 4, we identify methods for assessing specific life demands that can lead to stress.

The second half is devoted to methods for coping with and preventing stress. Chapter 5 offers a road map for understanding coping just as chapter 2 offers a road map for understanding stress. Chapter 6 offers suggestions for how to build coping resources such as wellness, relationship skills, tension-reduction practices, and ways of deepening spirituality. Chapter 7 examines stress-generating personalities, and chapter 8 suggests ways of overcoming stressful patterns of thinking. Chapter 9 reviews practices that create stress-free consciousness. And the last chapter, Chapter 10, is a concluding chapter that highlights key points and presents step-by-step instructions for using the many suggestions presented.

Part I

Understanding Stress

Chapter 1

The Phantom That Kills

*If you are distressed by anything external, the pain is not
due to the thing itself, but to your estimate of it; and this
you have the power to revoke at any moment.*

—Marcus Aurelius, Stoic philosopher
and Roman emperor, A.D. 120–180

"'It's just stress?' These headaches are real, and my back is killing
me! And all the doctor can say is, 'It's just stress.' I expected to get
some real help, not a lecture on how I need to relax and to take my
job less seriously. What does my doctor mean by *stress*, anyway?"

This scenario is common these days, as many medical practitioners have come to realize just how thin is the line between the mind

and the body. This acknowledgment is nothing short of a medical revolution, as physicians formerly were slow to recognize the impact of emotions on the functioning and health of the body. The role of anger, fear, depression, and other strong emotions in initiating or aggravating both physical and mental illness is now universally conceded.

Although his insight was not widely accepted in medical circles at the time, Harvard physiologist Walter B. Cannon (1936, p. 4) observed, "a highly important change has occurred in the incidence of disease. Serious infections have markedly decreased or almost disappeared . . . meanwhile, conditions involving strain in the nervous system have been greatly augmented." As medical science has reduced the incidence of infectious diseases, the slowly accumulating diseases of adaptation, that is, diseases fostered by unhealthy lifestyles, have become all too common. Hypertension, coronary heart disease, cerebral vascular accidents, ulceration, colitis, cancer, arthritis, headaches, lower back strain, and many other troublesome conditions result largely from lifestyle features, not the least of which is mismanaged stress and unhealthy habit patterns. What is needed now is not another pill or potion but better coping strategies and health habits.

While medical practitioners have been grappling with these new realities and the implications they have for our health, many of their patients remain in the dark. Many find it surprising that their attitudes, habits, and emotions could be responsible for their health problems. For them, stress is a featureless apparition, a phantom, a ghost. It doesn't seem real. After all, they are not wimps. They can handle the pressures of life. They are not going to cop out by claiming some kind of "stress" weakness. But stress is real, and one is not "wimping out" by recognizing the seriousness of sustained stress arousal and by taking steps to avoid it or to eliminate it. It is not a mark of good character to be stressed out! Being stressed out is, rather, evidence of a breakdown in your monitoring and coping skills. Taking preventive action to avoid the stress response appears wise indeed when you understand the extent to which the accompanying physiological changes threaten your health, happiness, and performance.

What Is Stress?

Before you can do something about stress, you must first understand what it is. The playwright Nigel Howard suggested that once you develop a theory of your own behavior, then you are free to disobey it. In the same way, once you have a good reading on the causes of your stress, it will become easier to avoid some stress and to manage the rest with the help of coping strategies we present in this book.

We all know what it feels like to be stressed out, but many people use the word *stress* without a clear definition of what the term really means. History isn't everyone's favorite subject, so we won't subject you to too much of it in this book. But just as our society has changed radically in the past hundred or so years, so have our notions about what stress is and how to respond to it. Therefore, to give you the most accurate picture of what is known about stress, we will take a brief look at how our emerging understanding of the stress process has changed in the past century. First, however, we'll provide a little language training about the terms that will be used throughout this book.

A Little Language Training

As our understanding of stress has changed, so has our terminology. At one point the term *stress* was applied in so many ways that its scientific usefulness was severely limited. It was first thought of as a source of pressure or strain on a person. Thus, it was common to say that one was under stress or that one was stressed. This is still the way most people refer to it. This usage of the term was first applied in physics, where it referred to the pressure applied to a material such as concrete or metal. If the stress placed on such materials is not too great, the molecules within the material will bounce back into formation after the stress is removed and, thus, the material will maintain its integrity. When the stress exceeds the resilient capacity of the material, however, permanent damage will be done. Analogously, it was said that humans, too, are resilient enough to

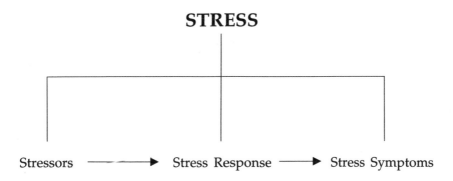

Figure 1-1. Relationships among stress terms.

spring back from most stressful situations. When the pressure exceeds their capacity to deal with it, however, they may experience significant disruption to their equilibrium. In the vernacular, they are said to "fall apart" or to have an "emotional breakdown."

With notable exceptions, the terms associated with stress have become somewhat standardized over time. *Stress* is now used as an umbrella concept covering all terms associated with the phenomenon. The *stress response* is the cascade of physiological, cognitive, and emotional changes that are incited by a stressful experience. *Stressors* are the environmental or internal events that instigate the stress response. And *stress symptoms* are the effects of the stress response on functioning. The relationships among these factors are depicted in Figure 1-1.

The Fight or Flight Syndrome

In the late eighteenth century Claude Bernard, the founder of modern experimental medicine, noted that each organism has an internal environment in which its organs and tissues live. He observed that in a healthy organism this internal environment remains essentially constant even when the external environment fluctuates considerably. In 1932 Cannon named the process by which the body maintains the constancy of this internal environment *homeostasis*. He further noted that anything that significantly disturbs this homeostatic state would activate a fight or flight syndrome, later to be called the stress response.

The General Adaptation Syndrome

Almost fifty years later, Hans Selye (1976), an endocrinologist, expanded our understanding of the fight or flight syndrome. found that rats that had been subjected to a wide array of stressful situations experienced the same set of physiological reactions. He maintained that this was true for humans as well. The exact nature of the stressor causing this reaction seems to be unimportant. The same neurological, hormonal, and immunological responses occur whether the stressor is road rage, news that your spouse wants a divorce, a sudden drop in the value of your stock portfolio, or the loss of a job. Although subsequent research demonstrated that the stress response was somewhat more specific than Selye held (Sapolsky 1998), the body's reaction to varied stressors appears to be similar across a wide gamut of stressors. Selye referred to the totality of the stress response as the *General Adaptation Syndrome*.

The General Adaptation Syndrome consists of three stages: Alarm, resistance, and exhaustion. You can think of these stages as similar to those a nation undergoes when faced with a military threat. Once a nation comes under attack, the alarm stage sets in. The threat is so shocking that the normal activities of its citizens are temporarily disrupted, as they become numb from the emotional trauma. The military's intelligence division processes the extent of the attack and devises strategic and tactical plans for resistance. The appropriate branches of the military are called into action, and citizens are reassured that all steps necessary to defeat the enemy are being taken. Faith in the resistance allows the citizens to return to their normal activities while the military engages the enemy. If the enemy overcomes the initial resistance, however, the resistance forces become exhausted, and the nation is once again thrust into alarm. At this point the nation has gone from alarm to resistance to exhaustion to alarm once again. During the second stage of alarm the military's intelligence once again assesses the situation and devises a second plan for resistance. The cycle from alarm to resistance to temporary exhaustion might repeat several times before victory is assured or the nation's defenses reach a final stage of exhaustion.

Similarly, when you are attacked by stressors, you experience the alarm stage, what Cannon called the fight or flight syndrome. Actually, the syndrome needs a slight modification, for your first reaction under threat is more likely to be freezing in place while you struggle to get an adequate reading of the stressor to decide on a course of resistance. Your resistance may take various forms, but quite often you will seek to withdraw or avoid the stressor rather than to fight. if your resistance strategy is effective, you will eliminate or lessen the effects of the stressor. If it is ineffective, you may temporarily experience exhaustion and recycle back into alarm again. You may recycle between alarm, resistance, and exhaustion several times before satisfactorily dealing with the stressor.

Stress as an Event

While Cannon and Selye were pioneers in explaining the way our bodies respond to threats in the environment, two physicians named Thomas Holmes and Richard Rahe revolutionized our understanding of the connection between life events and illness in the body. They developed the *Social Readjustment Rating Scale* (SRSS; Holmes and Rahe 1967) to measure the accumulation of various life events. Their research showed that scores on this scale were related to the possibilities of experiencing physical illness in the near future. On this scale, numeric weights are assigned to life events according to the level of unpleasantness or harmfulness each represents. For example, a catastrophic event such as the loss of a spouse has a weight of 100 (out of 100) on the scale, whereas relatively minor events such as taking out a loan for a major purchase has a weight of 17. The more "points" you accumulate in a short period, the greater chance you have of becoming sick from stress. Because this is an important starting place in understanding the stress you experience, we will return to their work in more detail in chapter 4 and provide you with the SRSS so that you can assess your own stresssors. We'll also discuss the work of West Coast researchers (Kanner, Coyne, Schaefer, and Lazarus 1981) who later found evidence that daily hassles—defined as daily interactions with the environment that were both negative and frequent—can be even more detrimental to your health than major events.

Transactional Models: Stress as a Psychological Balancing Act

We now know that objective measures of potentially stressful conditions such as unemployment, indebtedness, family members leaving home, changes in address, high noise levels, and the like are weak predictors of stress symptoms, because they discount personal reactions to these events. Indeed, researchers attempting to connect these types of life conditions to the occurrence of stress symptoms such as physical illness find a modest relationship at best (Rabkin and Struening 1976). Consequently, modern stress theories accord a pivotal role to personal variables that determine whether life demands will be viewed as stressors, challenges, or merely ordinary tasks requiring no emotional involvement.

Our current understanding of the stress process comes from researchers such as Richard Lazarus and Susan Folkman (1984), who see stress as the result of a *transaction* between the person and the environment—and not something that simply happens to you. According to Folkman and Lazarus, you conduct two fairly automatic mental operations when you encounter any potentially stressful event. First, you take stock of the potential threat posed by the event. They called this a "primary appraisal." Next, you conduct a sort of mental inventory of your resources for coping with the event, which they called a "secondary appraisal." Features of the demand (for example, its intensity and the perceived consequences of failure to deal successfully with it) and of resources (for example, their appropriateness and sufficiency) are all taken into consideration when appraising the seriousness of the situation. If you conclude that demands outstrip your resources, you become stressed out.

Perception Is the Key

The stress response, therefore, is triggered by the *perception* of real or imaginary loss, harm, or inadequacy. There is no stress *out there*. Out there are merely persons and events. Whether an event proves to be stressful or not depends on the meaning assigned to the event. One person's nightmare sometimes is another person's delight. For example, although sixty percent of Americans rate public speaking as being more terrifying than the prospect of imminent physical harm, others happily seek the opportunity to give formal speeches to live audiences.

It is not the news that stresses you but the editorials you write. The body doesn't know the difference between fact and fantasy when it comes to stress. It treats as reality whatever the mind gives it. Each time you perceive the likelihood of serious loss or harm, the body gears up stressfully, spewing out powerful stress hormones and bringing on lightning-like changes in the nervous system.

The most typical trigger to the stress response is the perception that your coping resources are inadequate for the demands you are facing. We are evaluating creatures. We constantly take measure of the demands we face and appraise the resources we possess for dealing with them. If the equation between perceived demands and perceived coping resources is nicely balanced, or better yet if your resources seem to be more substantial than the demands, you view the demands as mere challenges that offer you the opportunity to apply your skills and knowledge. If, however, the equation is imbalanced in favor of the demands, the demands become stressors and trigger the stress response. Challenges lead to healthy functioning and often help you to build additional coping resources. Chronic stressors, however, diminish the quality of your life.

The *intensity* of the stressful response depends on what you believe to be the consequences of failing to deal adequately with a demand. If you conclude that failing to cope successfully will not appreciably endanger your welfare, the stress response will be mild. On the other hand, if you believe that failure will have serious consequences for your job security, your marriage, your children, your reputation, or any other valuable interest, the stressful jolt is likely to be intense and lasting.

Over the years you develop certain beliefs about yourself, others, and the future. You filter your experiences through these beliefs. Some of them may have been established early in life, before your rational powers were well developed. You may have become conditioned to believe that the world is a threatening place, that the intentions of others are dishonorable, that it is best not to take on new challenges, or that it is dangerous to have others upset with you. Such beliefs become perceptual filters that can cause you to greatly overreact to life's challenges. You may take offense where no insult was intended. You may see murky figures lingering in the shadows. You may anticipate failure even before you begin the enterprise. And you worry, worry, and worry. Mark Twain once said, "I'm an old man, and I've seen many troubles in my days, most of which never happened." Bertrand Russell, the famous English philosopher, once became so unhappy with himself for worrying that he decided to keep a journal of events about which he worried. To his amazement he found that only 10 percent of the events he worried about ever occurred!

How often do you look to the future and give yourself a vote of no confidence? If you distrust your resources for coping, you may try to push the future into the past by anticipating possible harmful situations and dealing with them mentally *before* they happen. The actual events, whatever they are, are constantly being colored by the perceptual filters you have developed, and the attitudes to which they predispose you. James Branch Cabell (1926) wrote, "The optimist proclaims that we live in the best of all possible worlds; and the pessimist fears this is true." Pessimistic, self-sabotaging ways of reading your experiences automatically trigger the stress response. If, however, your past experiences have been self-enhancing, you may have developed a positive self-image that leads you to trust yourself, to give yourself a vote of confidence, and thus, to anticipate success and rewards.

These self-images are often formed early in your life. Social psychologists have suggested two ways they may be formed. Charles Cooley (1902), a social psychologist, maintained that you get your self-pictures from the way you are viewed by significant others. Daryle and Sandra Bem, prominent psychologists who have extensively studied the formation of gender roles, see it somewhat differently. They suggest that you get your self-concept from what you see yourself doing; that is, from your evaluations of your performances across a wide gamut of life's activities. It seems likely that Cooley's explanation of the origin of the self-concept is most appropriate for the childhood years. During these years the child's experiential base is too thin to challenge the views of parents, teachers, and other significant people. Consequently, children often accept uncritically the judgments of such people regarding their abilities and worth. Later, however, the Bems' view may come more into play. When you have had sufficient life experiences, you are in a position to fend off the negative views of others and to more competently judge your performance.

In other words, your overall self-impression probably stems from both the judgments of others and from your evaluations of your own performance. Either way, you develop perceptual frames through which you view life's demands and your resources. These perceptual frames are immensely important in determining the quality of the experiences you have, ideas we will cover more fully in chapter 4.

A Brief Example

So that you can get a more concrete picture of the role of perception in stress, let's look at the experiences of two executives who were subject to the same stressful company conditions and yet held radically different views of the situation. Their company had just merged with another company, and the inevitable thorny adjustments were being made. A consulting team had been called in to monitor the changes. The following are excerpts from the responses of the executives when asked for their views of what was going on.

Executive A

I have to tell you that, unfortunately, you could not have come to this company at a worse time. It's chaos here, no one knows what is going on, and you can't get good information. You also don't know who to go to for sign-offs and okays. You really can't get anything done. It's terrible here. I've never really seen anything like this before. So, I don't know what I can tell you that would be helpful. It's just a time of awful confusion and indirection. I'll try to help you as best I can, but I'm not sure there's much I can tell you.

Executive B

Welcome! You guys couldn't have come at a better time, let me tell you. It's total chaos around here. Nobody is in charge anymore. We're all trying to find our way and figure this out. Even the chain of command is a bit unclear, and you can't be sure who to go to for what, so you just go ahead and do what you think is best. You can get anything done you want, because there's nobody to stop you! We've had some ups and downs, but basically it's been a terrific time. I think this merger is going to end up being a great move. So I'm glad you came when you did. Now let's get to your questions.

It is clear from the different reactions of these two men to the same corporate conditions that stress results from the meaning we assign to our experiences. Executive A views changes within the corporation as catastrophic, as dangerously chaotic. As a result, he experiences a great deal of stress. The stress robs him of his energy. His work is no longer a challenge but becomes a stressor. He approaches it as though he were in an emotional crouch with arms folded in front of him to fend off the blows. In short, he experiences job burnout with the resulting emotional exhaustion and feelings of powerlessness.

In contrast, Executive B's version of what's going on in the corporation is altogether different. He sees conditions as highly promising. He sees the chaos as an opportunity to demonstrate leadership and creativity. The lack of direction and clear chain of command is interpreted to mean that constraints that sometimes stifle performance are absent, and he is free to experiment and create conditions for improved performance. As a result of his perception of the situation, he experiences exhilaration from the challenge that lies before his company. His energy abounds, his mood is buoyant, and his approach to problems is anticipatory and active.

Here we have the same situation, but the perceptions of the managers are significantly different. For Executive A, the conditions within the corporation forecast real trouble ahead, but for Executive B, they portend a rosy future. It is most telling that Executive B, Dan Burnham, went on to become CEO of a major U.S. corporation.

The Biology of Stress: A Response Whose Time Has Passed?

The stress response consists of massive, instantaneous, and reflexive physiological changes designed to prepare us to cope with acute physical emergencies. As we suggested in the preface, this super-preparedness likely was bred into our ancient ancestors at a time when they were exposed to constant danger. They had no technology to protect them from the elements, and they were often dinner for predators. They were hunted down by the tigers in the jungles and by the lions on the savannas. When a hungry predator was ready to spring, there was no time to contemplate the sunset, to digest a good meal, or even to objectively assess the approaching danger.

To survive the attack, a raft of physiological changes was necessary. A massive shot of adrenaline increased muscular readiness, heightened alertness, and energized the person either to do battle or escape—in other words, for "fight or flight." Neuropeptides and hormones flooded the body to orchestrate the mobilized condition. Digestion subsided to save energy for the battle. Muscles became taut to enhance performance. Sugar levels elevated to create the necessary fuel. The heartbeat quickened and the blood pressure rose to distribute fuel to muscles and the brain. Peripheral vision increased to detect impending blows from the left or right. Blood was routed away from the gastrointestinal tract to the muscles to facilitate action. Antidiuretic hormones caused the kidneys to preserve fluids to create more blood volume in case there was hemorrhaging. These and many other physiological changes occurred within seconds. Their purpose? To prepare the person to take action against an acute physical stressor.

Given the perilous conditions our ancestors faced, it is little wonder that natural selection favored those who were a bit paranoid and hyper-vigilant, who were constantly looking over their shoulders for predators. All the laid-back types were eaten up, and the only ones left to pass along their genes were a bunch of nervous Nellies. As a legacy these ancestors left us a nervous system that is greatly overreactive to the very different demands associated with modern living.

It's All in Your Head

The physiology of the stress response is quite amazing. The chain of events leading to the stress response begins with an alerting signal that is sent to the thalamus, a brain structure that sorts out incoming signals and sends them to the brain's cortex. The cortex draws upon its gigantic memory bank of past experiences to properly interpret the signal. If potential harm or loss is anticipated, the cortex causes the amygdala, another brain structure, to create stressful emotional arousal and triggers the hypothalamus to initiate a series of biochemical and nervous system changes that create the stress response. More specifically, the hypothalamus triggers the pituitary gland to release a powerful hormone (ACTH) that is picked up in the adrenal glands causing them to produce corticoids. These corticoids play a major role in preparing the body for stressful reactions. They reduce inflammation throughout the body to allow for smoother functioning of muscles, cause the liver to raise blood-sugar levels for fuel, and increase blood volume. At the same time the sympathetic nervous system and adrenal glands produce epinephrine and norepinephrine that increase the heart and breathing rates and speed up the rate at which nerve cells send messages.

In short, our initial understanding of the stress response was as follows:

1. Stressful signals are sent to the thalamus from where they are directed to the cortex for evaluation.

2. If the signals are judged to be threatening, the cortex causes

   a. the amygdala to arouse the emotions and

   b. the hypothalamus to cause the pituitary gland, the adrenal glands, and the sympathetic nervous systems to produce biochemicals that create the stress response.

The Startle Response

Recent breakthroughs in neuroscience, however, require a change in our understanding of this chain of events. In 1984 Joseph LeDoux discovered a direct neural connection between the thalamus and the amygdala. So, the thalamus is able to send signals directly to the amygdala to trigger the stress response *before* its signal to the cortex arrives. This direct route from the thalamus to the amygdala is like a neural tripwire that bypasses the more thoughtful part of the brain and reflexively starts the stress reaction. From signals arriving through this "neural back alley," the amygdala is able to initiate an emotional reaction to incoming signals before the higher thought processes of the cortex have been able to more fully evaluate the signal. It seems the body is equipped to begin the stress response without you—that is, without the active participation of the thinking brain.

Clearly this is the route taken by the "startle response." If while walking through the woods a snake drops onto your shoulder from an overhanging branch, you are not likely to cognitively process information about the snake before experiencing the startle response and frantically throwing it to the ground. For some time afterwards you are likely to feel your heart race, your muscles tightening, your blood rushing to your head. The experience dominates your thinking and emotions. Daniel Goleman (1994) refers to this primitive, reflexive reaction that usurps your attention and emotions as *emotional hijacking*.

Given the threatening conditions under which early humans most likely lived, it is easy to understand the survival value of this more direct route to stress arousal. Even a few milliseconds might make a difference in the ability to react to a predator. It appears that nature was willing to have us unnecessarily aroused again and again to insure that we would be properly prepared for the real threat when it occurred.

Stressful Conditioning

Some emotional experiences may condition you to neurotically react to situations, events, or objects that, in reality, constitute no threat at all. Such unfortunate conditioning can cause a great deal of stress if the conditioned stimuli are often present in everyday life. Agoraphobia is an excellent example of such conditioning. The panicky reactions of agoraphobic patients often are set off by such common experiences as driving on freeways, shopping along the wide isles of supermarkets, or just being outside the home. The resulting limitations may cripple their ability to participate fully in the activities of daily living. This punishing conditioning can be eliminated by procedures discussed in chapter 8.

In acute physical emergencies, therefore, the body doesn't wait for you to ponder the seriousness of the situation; it takes matters into its own hands to allow for a more timely reaction. In less acute situations, however, the role of appraisal—the conscious, thoughtful evaluation of the situation—becomes critical in determining your responses. As we will see, both the reflexive action of the neural tripwire (thalamus → amygdala) *and* the deliberative action of the brain's higher thought processes have important roles to play.

The Stress Response: A Modern-Day Hazard

The stress response that was so useful during the human family's infancy has become a major hazard to our health. Now and then there are occasions where the extra energy and sharpened senses the stress response provides may prove to be life saving. For example, in 1982 a spectator dove into the icy waters of the Potomac River near a Washington, D.C., airport to drag to safety passengers of a crashed Air Florida airliner. And some years back there was the case of a petite mother who lifted the rear of a pickup truck off the abdomen of her three-year-old son who had been run over. But for the most part the fight or flight response is a throwback to primitive eras, an evolutionary hangover. Because we seldom face the kind of physical danger for which the stress response was designed, it is seldom appropriate for modern life. In fact, the stress response may now constitute a greater threat to our survival than the perceived threats that trigger it. It is analogous to the allergic response. The allergen that triggers the allergic reaction presents no actual threat to the person's well-being. It is the body's unnecessary defense reaction that is the threat. This inflammation swells the nasal membranes, clogs the air tract with mucous discharge, causes breathing difficulty, and generally makes us feel miserable.

Similarly, most stress responses are totally unnecessary. Imagine for example that you work for a company that has been laying off its workers. Now imagine that one of your closest friends has just received a pink slip. It's not hard to imagine your reaction. You may feel anger at the company for letting him go and perhaps fear regarding your own security with the company. "It's not fair," you say. "Don't the higher-ups care at all about us? After giving the best years of your life to this company, when it suits their purpose they lay you off without any consideration. What's my friend to do now?"

Just thinking about the situation makes your pulse quicken, the muscles in your back and neck tense up, and your heart pound. These symptoms may persist for days, along with sleeplessness, changes in your appetite, the whole nine yards. There are two realities here: One, your reactions are perfectly understandable, and two, your stressful reactions will likely do nothing at all to improve the lot of either your friend or yourself.

No matter what you tell yourself or other people, life has its share of unpleasant events, and you are going to react to them physically, mentally, and emotionally. We seem especially well suited to plan for an endless list of things that may go wrong in the future. Actually, many of us spend a great deal of energy being concerned about things that have very *little* chance of happening. Perhaps this even explains why—even in a society in which many of us have access to material resources unheard of in human history—drugs such as Prozac make billions for pharmaceutical companies, levels of depression and suicide remain high, and the main goal of many forms of entertainment is to distract us from the realities of day-to-day life.

Despite the grave threats you may perceive in your world, most situations that initiate the stress response today are threats to your *ego*, not to your body. Unfortunately, the fight-flight readiness of the stress response is counterproductive in handling such threats. At the very least, the unnecessary arousal interferes with clear thinking, wastes your energy, and drains your emotions. At worst, it imperils your health, lowers your work performance, interrupts your relationships with others, and in general erodes the quality of your life. Prolonged stress arousal is now believed to play a causal or exacerbating role in hypertension, stroke, coronary heart disease, ulcers, migraine headaches, tension headaches, cancer, allergies, asthma, rheumatoid arthritis, backaches, and the TMJ syndrome (Greenberg 1999).

And Now For Some Good News: We Can Tame the Human Nervous System

The good news is that you really can do something about reducing your stress. The ultimate stress management strategy would be the taming of the human nervous system—that is, to master your body's reactions to external demands so that you can cope effectively with modern life. Many Americans already attempt to do this, but unfortunately, they attempt it through chemistry at 6 o'clock happy hours or through the frequent use of tranquilizing drugs. Certainly, there are situations in which chemical interventions can be helpful, but often you underestimate your capacities for coping without resorting to such means. Or, if you have not developed these capacities, you underestimate the potential for improving your life by developing them. A headache is not your body's way of telling you it needs more aspirin! It is telling you that something is impinging on your well-being and needs to be remedied.

Your experience of stress is actually the result of an interaction of events, your manner of interpreting them, and the resources you possess for coping with them. This interaction can occur in an instant, however. When a hungry tiger is charging, you don't have time for extended deliberations. But that's the problem for most of us today: You don't need to have your body and mind in the alarm stage to prepare for a tax audit, but that's exactly what's likely to happen when you open that letter from the IRS. Worse, the heightened readiness of your body can exact a tremendous toll on your physical and emotional well-being which, of course, not only makes you feel bad but also renders you less capable of managing your life.

Over the last several decades, professionals who are interested in human stress have learned a great deal about how we cope with life's demands, and much of it has not been communicated to the general public in a systematic way. The time seems right to suggest a more comprehensive guide to managing stressful situations and events. In the following chapter, we will examine some of the demands of modern living that contribute to stress. Next, we offer a "road map for stress." Like a typical road map, this one will contain routes—routes by which ordinary life changes may trigger stressful reactions. Understanding how stress is triggered is essential to developing effective means of coping.

Chapter 2

The Escalating Demands of Modern Living

"A slow sort of country!" said the Queen. "Now, here, you see, it takes all the running you can do, to keep in the same place. If you want to get somewhere else, you must run at least twice as fast as that!"

—Lewis Carroll, *Alice in Wonderland*

Many Americans must feel as though they live in the country of Lewis Carroll's Queen, for it seems to take all the running they can do just to keep in the same place. The dizzying demands of modern living push many people to the limits of their coping abilities. Robert Kegan, senior lecturer at the Harvard Graduate School of Education, suggests in his book *In Over Our Heads* (1994) that the mental requirements of modern life constitute a "hidden curriculum"—a bewildering array of expectations, prescriptions, claims, and demands. In many cases the culture's curriculum proves to be too tough to pass. Take, for instance, Joyce, a living example of a person being crunched by multiple demands and responsibilities.

Joyce was experiencing a mild, chronic form of depression that had lasted for about a year. In the beginning, she was at a loss to explain why she felt so listless, and so helpless in overcoming her feelings. Joyce was an extremely bright and capable woman who grew up in relative poverty in the South. She had overcome many obstacles in her life and had a strong personal belief in individual accountability and responsibility. At the time that she entered counseling, Joyce was enrolled as a full-time student and was making all As. She also worked twenty to thirty hours per week as a nurse and was a wife and mother of three young children. She usually got by on a few hours sleep, often studied until the early morning hours, had very little time with her children or husband, and at the end of a long week usually faced several twelve-hour shifts working in the hospital. Given what we've discussed so far about stress, it would be more surprising if Joyce *wasn't* depressed. Who could be happy when faced with such taxing demands?

Fortunately for Joyce, her circumstances were somewhat temporary. She was in school because she was planning on switching careers. Joyce's ultimate goal was to leave the nursing profession and become a public interest lawyer. Over the course of about six months in counseling, she was gradually able to cut back on her external demands as well as to develop her own capacities for coping. She worked on overcoming her perfectionism as a student and found that she could indeed live with 95 percent on her tests instead of 100s. Even more importantly, she could use the extra time she previously channeled into being a perfect student to be with her family. She also found ways to cut back on the hours she was working as a nurse and still managed to make ends meet. It would have been a tremendous mistake to ignore the very real external pressures Joyce was facing, and it took time and patience for her to craft a lifestyle that was somewhat less demanding on her time and energy. As she did so, she felt her depression lift, and she began to take pleasure once again in her daily activities. One of her biggest breakthroughs in counseling came when she was able to visit a local mall for no other reason than to goof off!

The point of Joyce's story, of course, is that she was suffering from an overdose of life demands, and despite her considerable capacity for coping, her waning emotional health forced her to slow down. Although her intentions and goals were laudable, Joyce suffered from a very common American malady: trying to lead the lives of three or four people at once. Some of us choose this lifestyle. We want to "be all that we can be," and be the best at whatever we do. Today that means working long hours to get ahead, no matter if you are talking about school, work, or athletics. However, others lead demanding lives because they *feel they have no choice*, a condition likely to be much more harmful.

Stressful Lives of Luxury

So far, we have introduced you to some of the current thinking about what stress is and how it operates in our lives. And we have suggested that while the stress response was once vital to our survival, in modern times it is often a threat to our well-being. But many people still find this idea hard to accept. How is it possible that stress can exact such a terrible toll on a society that has amassed so many comforts and conveniences? Some even maintain that we have developed a culture of self-indulgent narcissists, that we are so spoiled by our many luxuries we have lost touch with what it means to "really" experience stress.

It is true of course that human beings quickly become accustomed to new conveniences. Air-conditioners used to be something of a novelty, but today they are often considered to be essential utilities. It still feels good when you enter the local shopping mall and that blast of cold air first hits you, but after a few minutes you adapt and more or less take this pleasant environment for granted. The same is true for almost every other quality-of-life improvement: at first it is exciting, but it soon becomes ordinary, and then it gets taken for granted. As Ralph Waldo Emerson wrote, "A luxury soon becomes a necessity."

In a material sense, our lives have been enriched on a scale unimaginable to people living a hundred years ago. In the last century, most industrial nations experienced tremendous technological advances that have become commonplace for the great majority of their citizens. The average American at the beginning of the twenty-first century has access to goods and services beyond the reach of even the richest individual living a hundred years ago: travel across the oceans in a matter of hours, instant worldwide communications, and portable computers capable of running all manner of software programs and connecting to millions of other computers through the Internet. Upon hearing of such innovations, a time traveler from a century ago would likely conclude that we are all living in some sort of utopian paradise. As recently as the 1960s World's Fair in New York, a twenty-hour work week was promised, and as late as the mid 1980s many counselors thought that the number-one health issue of the future would be finding ways to fill up our leisure time. So what went wrong?

The Mismatch of Culture and Physiology

How can it be that despite the tremendous material resources we have accumulated and the unprecedented heights we have achieved in fields such as science, medicine, and technology, many people still lead lives of great stress? The key is this: The nature of stress today is *psychological*, not *physical*. Our ancient forebears confronted instantaneous, concrete threats: aggression from predatory animals, tribal warfare, the specter of starvation, and vulnerability to the elements. Over time they developed a physical preparedness to deal with these threats that we now call the stress response. However, this response is not as well suited to the demands of modern living. Because of our tremendous progress, few of us face the immediate physical threats commonly experienced by our ancestors. Most of today's demands are psychosocial in nature, but our bodies still respond in the same physiological way: preparation for fight or flight.

A. T. W. Simeons (1961) in *Man's Presumptuous Brain* noted that the evolution of our cultures has far outstripped the evolution of our bodies. The laws, codes, ordinances, and manners that currently govern human interactions have become more and more civilized over the eons, whereas the human nervous system is a throwback to a primordial era. When a coworker or supervisor berates you at work, you have a similar physiological response to animals in the wild—your blood starts boiling, stress hormones pump through your body, your muscles tighten—but you have no acceptable outlet for it. You must find other ways to cool down the body's natural response to stress.

Handling stress successfully becomes even more important when you realize that although our material circumstances have improved remarkably, we still confront many demands. You may face the possibility of being downsized at work. Your community may be beset by crime and underfunded public services. You may be a victim of natural disasters. The list goes on and on, and thanks to modern forms of communication, you can see and hear the troubles of the entire world daily on the news. Your body's first response to all of this is the same as if a hungry tiger were charging you: It mobilizes for action. Unfortunately, in a modern world, such mobilization is worse than useless. It not only lessens your ability to solve complex problems, but it eventually wears the body down, creating additional sources of stress.

A key point in coping with stress is that you have a choice in assigning meaning to your experiences. It is generally adaptive to interpret situations in the most benign manner possible. For example, you can often stress yourself out by attributing negative intentions to the people whom you encounter. "Was the clerk at the store *really* doing all she could to help me find my brand of toothpaste?" "Why can't my landlord get the leak in my faucet fixed?" "Does my boss understand how hard I worked to get that project done on time?" Often, you can never truly confirm or disprove your suspicions regarding the intentions of others, leaving you in the dark about other people's perceptions and motives. Your life is likely to be significantly happier if you form the habit of making generous, humane assumptions regarding the motives of others.

Although you often add to your own stress by seeing imaginary phantoms in every dark corner, it is important to recognize *real* pressures when they are present. Although we emphasize the considerable freedom you have in interpreting your experiences, we don't suggest for a minute that your problems are not the result of real and mounting pressures you face in the modern world. Indeed, there is much evidence that for many people, life is becoming more complex, more burdensome, and more demanding.

However, without a clear reading on the demands you face, it is extremely difficult to cope effectively. The purpose of this chapter is to identify some of the major demands of modern living that often challenge your ability to cope effectively. Unlike the tigers of centuries gone by, the invisible tigers of today are often chronic, ambiguous, and social in nature. This is both bad news and good news. The bad news is that such stressors are likely to last much longer. The good news is you have more time to choose and apply your coping resources. Just as the nature of most stressors is psychological, so is the solution. By recognizing the mixed blessings of modern living, you are better able to soak up the positive experiences and to sidestep the negative ones. You can't do this perfectly, of course, but you can *do it better*. But first, you need to understand these demands for what they are.

Technology Takes a Toll

Although many factors shape our lifestyles in the twenty-first century, modern technology has had perhaps the greatest influence over how we lead our lives. It is almost impossible to imagine how different our lives would be without the various machines, gadgets, appliances, and devices we rely on. We sleep in temperature-controlled houses, wake to alarm clocks, prepare our meals with various appliances, and drive to work in automobiles. Increasing numbers of workers spend much of their day in front of computers, performing various tasks and communicating with coworkers by e-mail. At the end of the day, we get back in our automobiles, and perhaps spend a few hours of recreation watching television or videotapes. At bedtime, we shut down our electrical fiefdoms until day breaks again.

Few would argue the fact that life in the United States in the new millennium is becoming more and more complicated. Information is available at the speed of light through media such as television and the Internet. We now have access to a worldwide communications network that offers the potential for instant access to anyone anywhere in the world. Although many of these technologies promise to simplify and enhance our lives, what they deliver can be just the opposite: the burden that comes with being immediately available to anyone at the touch of a button. Advertisements for these devices promise the freedom to roam anywhere and still be in touch, the security of being able to call for assistance if your car breaks down on some lonely highway, and perhaps even the prestige of being important enough to deserve such attention. However, instead of freeing you up, modern communication devices may actually tether you to other people. Cellular phones, fax machines, and digital pagers can blur the distinction between home and work, day and night, weekday and weekend.

Certainly, revolutionary advances such as the Internet offer a great many obvious advantages. The same is true in other fields. Modern medicine has banished many communicable diseases. Modern agriculture has wiped out starvation for the great majority of the citizens living in technologically advanced countries. Modern outlets for media allow you to sample the very best that our culture has to offer, from movies to music to sports to literature. But it is increasingly obvious that almost every technological advance brings with it some hidden, or not so hidden, drawbacks. Though it seems that everything about new technology is designed to bring people together and lighten our loads, this is obviously not always the case.

Technological Isolation

The speed and complexity of modern communication systems seems almost inversely related to personal intimacy. Much of the computer software available today is designed to draw you into the computer and away from other people. Of course, some innovations bridge gaps between people. E-mail and computer chat rooms allow instant access to people all over the world at the touch of a few buttons. However, you have to ask whether this expands your communication network or simply replaces it. In other words, do such technologies take away from your time with friends and family in your immediate environment and replace them with strangers? How many people spend hours every night communicating with distant strangers they will never meet, even though they barely speak to people who live only a few yards away in their own neighborhood?

The electronic highway that facilitates telecommunication at lightning speed may lessen the opportunities for real, face-to-face contact with others and can lead to social isolation. In this way you may lose one of the most effective resources we have for dealing with stress—each other! The use of these devices tends to take priority over interchanges with real people. Even in supermarkets, customers walk the aisles with cell phones glued to their ears, presumably adding to shopping lists they hurriedly assembled before leaving the house. So we may be talking more and relating less.

Some have suggested that technology can isolate you not only from your surroundings but even your own consciousness. Tor Norretranders, a science writer from Denmark, suggested in his bestseller *The User Illusion* (1998) that in any given second, you consciously process only about sixteen of the eleven million bits of information your senses pass on to the brain. Your mind is capable of narrowing your consciousness to interactions with other people and to your work, making you blissfully unaware of the rich sensory environment in which you live. At other times, such as when taking a leisurely walk through the neighborhood or even taking a vacation to the Grand Canyon, you may allow yourself to be much more open to this sensory information. Norretranders suggests, however, that many modern forms of work and entertainment sharply reduce the amount of input you receive. Even though computers operate at high speeds and come equipped with sophisticated sound and video systems, the relative trickle of information that reaches you through the computer screen may actually represent a form of sensory deprivation.

Demands in the Workplace

In 1851, English social critic John Ruskin wrote that three things were necessary for people to be happy in their work: a) they needed to have the necessary skills and abilities, b) they must have a sense of success in it, and c) they must not do too much. Today, the U.S. workplace is marked by kaleidoscopic changes that present a challenge to each of Ruskin's recommendations: corporate downsizing; pervasive job insecurity; ever-expanding work hours; the need for continual retooling to keep pace with the introduction of new technology; the tethering of workers to their jobs through electronic mail, beepers, cell phones and laptops; telecommuting; and the shrinking of worker benefits.

Competitive pressures from the global market make constant demands for increased worker productivity. Despite the recent strength of the U.S. economy, whether or not this prosperity is felt by the average American is suspect. The gulf between the haves and have-nots has grown increasingly wide in the past several decades: the incomes of the top 1 percent of wage earners more than doubled between 1979 and 1989 at the same time that the bottom 20 percent of earners saw their incomes fall by 10 percent (Krugman 1992). Opportunity in the United States used to be represented by jobs in the trades or manufacturing, which did not necessarily require extended formal education but offered hardworking individuals the chance to learn a profession, earn a decent wage, and eventually be promoted. However, today those jobs are disappearing, and increasingly the U.S. workforce is composed of a relatively small number of high-paying jobs that require extensive education and training, and a larger number of jobs in the services that require little training but offer low wages, little job security, and narrow prospects for advancement.

Off to Work We Go

Even so, today we work harder and more productively than at any time in the history of the world, and these trends shows no signs of abating as we begin the twenty-first century. In medieval France and England, the workday for peasants may have stretched from dawn to dusk during peak harvest times, but they may have worked only 120 days of the year, and their long work days were interspersed with mealtimes, naps, and breaks. Juliet Schor described the phenomenon of increasing work hours in her book, *The Overworked American: The Unexpected Decline of Leisure:*

> Since 1948, [the] productivity [of the American worker] has failed to rise in only five years. The level of productivity of the U.S. worker has more than doubled. In other words, we could now produce our 1948 standard of living (measured in terms of marketed goods and services) in less than half the time it took in that year. We actually could have chosen the four-hour day. Or a working year of six months. Or, every worker in the United States could now be taking every other year off from work—with pay (1992, p. 2).

Schor notes that instead of decreasing, the time that Americans spend at work has risen steadily over the past several decades. For a long time, the United States paralleled Western European countries in the ratio of work-to-leisure time, but since World War II, we have headed in opposite directions. Schor (1992) points out that the average U.S. manufacturing employee works an extra 320 hours (equivalent to two months) beyond his counterpart in West Germany and France. Even compared to our own recent past, we are working harder. Schor estimated that in the time span from 1969 to 1987, the average employed worker spent an additional 163 hours at work, the equivalent of one extra month. She also noted that such trends seem remarkably broad-based across different income levels and family patterns.

Schor also points to a gender gap in these results: during the same period, men put in an additional 98 hours per week while women did 305 additional hours. These statistics obviously reflect the increasing tendency of women to enter the paid workforce: in 1950, fewer than one-fourth of married women were in the workforce, whereas today more than 58 percent of married women work, and 75 percent of them are employed full-time. Women who have young children are also increasingly employed outside the home: in 1950, only 12 percent of women with preschool children worked, while today 60 percent are employed. And it's not as though men have cut back on their work loads either: thirty percent of men with children under fourteen report working fifty or more hours per week, and the same percentage also work on the weekends at their regular employment. Many others use the weekend to work a second job.

All of these trends obviously have the potential to create higher levels of stress. For many workers, the line separating work and home life has been badly blurred. Electronic networking allows employees to continue working on their mushrooming job assignments at home, after returning from a long day at the office. Consequently, the quality and quantity of time spent with family and friends may suffer badly, social support systems may weaken, and opportunities for deriving meaning from community service may decline as well. We have become a twenty-four-hour society capable of working around the clock. Advances in technology have made our work easier to do, but as a result we are now expected to produce more and work longer hours.

Work: A Hazard to Your Health?

So it is no secret that work has the potential to contribute greatly to your stress. We have already devoted a significant portion of this chapter to some of the reasons work stress is a problem for increasing numbers of Americans. However, to successfully manage this stress, it's important to get a clear reading on its exact source.

Manning, Curtis, and McMillen (1999) list five trends that threaten workers' health in their book, *Stress: Living and Working in a Changing World*. We'll summarize the trends here because they provide a good overview of stress-related issues in the workplace.

1. *New technology.* The nature of work is constantly changing. The introduction of computers into the workplace represented nothing less than a revolution in the way that work is conducted. Most workers use one in some way, no matter what their occupations. The increasing emphasis on technology in the workplace has changed the way that companies do business, not to mention expectations for employees. Decades ago, many companies were willing to hire capable workers and provide them training. But it has become increasingly expected that workers are already proficient in computer applications before they are hired. Many workers are now able to telecommute from home and never set foot in the office except for the occasional meeting. Some experts worry that technology creates a rift in the workforce between a few highly trained, highly paid workers and much larger numbers of those without such skills, who are often relegated to low-paying, low-status jobs without much prospect for advancement.

2. *Workforce diversity.* Many of the social changes that began with the reform movements of the 1960s have led to an increasingly diverse workforce. This diversity includes not only gender and ethnicity, but also sexual orientation, age, and those with disabilities. Diversity is also reflected in the increasingly broad array of skills, abilities, and interests necessary in today's economy. Today's workers must learn to interact with coworkers from very different backgrounds and possibly reexamine some of the "old rules" for relationships in the workplace. Although many of these social changes are long overdue, they nevertheless can create high levels of stress.

3. *Global competition.* International competition brought about by technological innovation brings with it both the pressure to perform and a fear of "outsiders." International trading bodies such as the World Trade Organization have been the subject of much political debate. Manning et al. (1999) cited a report in *Time* stating that in the 1960s only 7 percent of the U.S. economy was exposed to international competition, a figure that grew to 70 percent in the 1980s and is expected to continue climbing.

4. *Organizational restructuring.* The phenomenon of corporate restructuring, including corporate mergers, takeovers, and downsizing, created both intense media coverage and high levels of fear and uncertainty. Many workers treated such developments as synonymous with decreased wages or outright dismissals. Temporary or part-time workers are becoming an increasing part of the workforce. At the close of the twentieth century, Manpower International, a temporary employment agency, overtook General Motors to become America's largest employer. Many workers at the lower echelons of restructured corporations often resent the highly placed executives who seem to benefit generously from such activities.

5. *Changing work systems.* There seems to be an emerging redefinition of work itself. Rather than on the function of one's specific occupation or title, the focus in the workplace is increasingly on the unique set of skills and abilities each worker possesses. Many companies, forced to deal with changes in technology, consumer demands, and international competition, are increasingly turning to innovative methods for accomplishing work.

To successfully negotiate such changes, it is important to get a clear reading on the exact nature of the demands that might be causing you the most trouble. Below is a checklist of seven factors related to work stress that Barnett and Rivers (1996) identified from their research. Read each and indicate whether it is currently a source of stress for you at work.

1. **Work skills.** Does your job entail sufficient complexity and challenge in the type of skills you use and do you feel comfortable in using these skills? _____ yes _____ no

2. **Decision authority.** Do you have reasonable authority to make the decisions necessary to perform your job? _____ yes _____ no

3. **Schedule control.** Do you have reasonable control over the hours you work? _____ yes _____ no

4. **Job demands.** Do you have reasonable control over the number of tasks you perform at work, the time allotted to accomplish them, and the number of conflicting demands placed on your time? _____ yes _____ no

5. **Pay adequacy.** Is your pay adequate compared to others doing the same work? _____ yes _____ no

6. **Job security.** Are you reasonably certain that you won't be fired or "downsized" in the near future?

_____ yes _____ no

7. **Relations with supervisor.** Do you get along well with your supervisor?   _____ yes _____ no

Answering "no" to even one of these questions may mean that your work has the potential to be a significant source of stress for you. If you answered "no" to several of the items, it is likely that your work is already causing you difficulty. Left unchecked, such stress can escalate into a more severe condition known as work *burnout*.

The End of the Line: Worker Burnout

The term burnout was originally a concept from the field of space engineering. This early usage term is reflected in *Webster's Third New International Dictionary* definition of *burnout* as "the moment at which a jet or rocket motor exhausts its fuel." As a topic of scientific inquiry, work burnout is a relatively new concept. Though the idea itself is hardly new, its emergence as a distinct concept did not occur until the 1970s. The term "work burnout" was first used by Herbert Freudenberger (1974), a New York psychiatrist who noticed that his once idealistic and highly motivated clinical staff suffered from a gradual loss of energy, motivation, and commitment, mental and physical exhaustion, and a wide range of physical and emotional symptoms.

Given the rampant stressful conditions in the workplace, it is not surprising that the concept of job burnout has received increasing attention recently. Over the past twenty years, the term burnout has changed from a cavalier reference to the typical, hectic week at the office to a topic of scientific inquiry with a significant place in stress literature.

In the most commonly cited definition of burnout, Maslach and and Schaufeli (1993) describe it as a syndrome with three dimensions. These dimensions include depersonalization (distancing oneself from others and viewing others impersonally); reduced personal accomplishment (devaluing one's accomplishments in working with others); and emotional exhaustion (feeling emptied of personal emotional resources and becoming highly vulnerable to stressors). Burnout can also be distinguished from work stress and depression. The difference between burnout and work stress is that burnout is a breakdown in adaptation to prolonged work stress accompanied by emotional exhaustion and cynicism. Burnout results from exposure to chronic work stressors and not from stressors that are traumatic in nature or stressors that evolve out of major life events. There is substantial overlap between depression and emotional exhaustion, but not with the other two dimensions of the burnout syndrome, depersonalization and reduced personal accomplishment. Further, burnout, unlike depression, necessarily has its origins in the job setting and is characterized by cynicism. Manning et al. (1999) provide the following formula for work burnout:

> Too many demands on energy and resources over a long period of time

+

> High expectations for your performance and a deep commitment to your work

+

> Few actions taken to replenish your capacities

If you answered "no" to several of the items in the preceding work quiz, and if the formula above seems to characterize your approach to work, your chances of experiencing burnout may be very high. But one's work and personal life are never completely separate: each influences and is dependent on the other. In the following section, we will examine connections between one's personal and work life.

Balancing Work and Personal Life

> *The intellect of man is forced to choose*
> *Perfection of the life, or of the work,*
> *And if it take the second must refuse*
> *A heavenly mansion, raging in the dark.*
> *When all that story's finished, what's the news?*
> *In luck or out, the toil has left its mark:*
> *That old perplexity, an empty purse,*
> *Or the day's vanity, the night's remorse.*

—William Butler Yeats "The Choice"

As the Irish poet Yeats makes clear, it's tough to balance a personal life with a career. As another saying goes, some of us live to work and some work to live. Very few of us would be happy devoting ourselves exclusively to our work, although many people end up doing just that. But many highly successful people at the zenith of their careers find themselves stricken with feelings of despair after they have reached the top of the mountain. They look around, and ask, "Is that all there is?" However, it seems far too simplistic to suggest that you can simply "put family first." How can you do that when you have financial obligations that can only be met by earning a living? Studs Terkel chronicled the lives of everyday American workers in his 1975 book, *Working*, and concluded that work "is by its very nature about violence—to the spirit as well as the body . . . to survive the day is triumph enough for the walking wounded among a great many of us."

Changes in the way we work are inextricably bound with our personal lives. Chronicling the travail of the modern family seems to be one of the staples of evening news programs such as NBC's *Dateline* or CBS's *48 Hours*. These segments often highlight the difficulties experienced by parents struggling to maintain careers and families, and you are often treated to documentary-style footage of their daily routines. You watch tired parents rising at the crack of dawn to get children ready for school and to get themselves ready for work. They work hard all day, perhaps into the late evening. In the meantime, their children go to an aftercare program, unless they are old enough to become "latch-key" children. Often, in dual-career families, parents work in shifts, one working in the day and the other at night. Obviously, they are exhausted at the end of the day and may have little energy left over to share the day's experiences with each other. And these are the routine days—heaven help them if someone is sick or needs extra attention! Even though these scenes increasingly seem to be the norm for many Americans, few solutions are offered. Bills have to be paid and children have to be taken care of, and the daily grind seems to be the only game in town. The only hope seems to be to earn and save enough money so that one day they can afford to enjoy life a little, but for many such promises can seem tenuous and far-off at best.

One of the network news magazines, conducting a series of profiles on modern families, provided a poignant example of this grind. The particular couple portrayed had recently had a new baby. The father worked as a mechanic and the mother had left the workforce to have her baby. This family was being profiled because the mother had recently decided to start work again to help them get over the financial bind they were experiencing. To do this, they were forced to place their young child in day care, and of course, both parents had to do considerable juggling to make sure one of them could pick up the child when the day-care center closed or stay home when the child was sick.

It goes without saying that both parents (and presumably the child as well) experienced considerable stress in trying to balance working outside the home with raising a small child on a limited budget. As part of the broadcast, the network employed a financial advisor to analyze the economic trade-offs the family had made by having both parents work. This financial advisor added up the costs and benefits associated with the mother starting work again, and showed that the family actually *lost* money when the mother started work! In addition to the emotional strain of having to leave the child with others during the day and the demands of two people balancing their jobs, the family was actually taking a financial hit in the process.

How could this be? For one, full-time day care can be expensive, ranging anywhere from $300 to $600 a month or more. In addition, with two parents working, the family often paid more when they shopped than before, because they had little time or energy to bargain hunt, clip coupons, or look for sales. The father also had to cut back on overtime when the mother started work so he could be home with his child when his wife was at work. When all of these expenses were subtracted from the extra income the mother was making at work, they actually lost money. The news magazine piece ended by showing the grief and sadness the couple experienced when these facts were laid out and they realized how they were losing at both ends of this bargain.

The point of this example is not that it is wrong for two parents to work, that the mother is the parent who should stay home with the child, or that day care is not in a child's best interests. The point is that you need a clear reading on your demands if you are to cope effectively. Surely if this couple knew this information at the outset, they would not have put themselves through months of anguish that separated them from their child and lost them money in the process. But it is easy to see how they ended up in this predicament. You hear about the necessity of two incomes all the time in the media, but you hear little about alternative ways of making ends meet. You more or less take for granted that the way to cope with financial hardship these days is to work more hours, not cut back on your expenses. Advertisers who want you to buy their products fund the news programs that document these types of difficulties. The occasional portrayals of families finding creative ways to cut back on spending are dwarfed by commercials hawking the newest minivans, appliances, clothing, and the like. This brings us to our next modern source of stress: lack of time.

Time Squeeze

Many Americans are feeling a serious time squeeze. During the "Work, Stress, and Health '99 Conference" sponsored by the

American Psychological Association, psychologist Steven Sauter reported that professionals studying family life not so long ago referred to "time overload," then later to "time poverty," and finally to "time famine." In a recent book titled *Faster: The Acceleration of Just About Everything*, author James Gleick (1999) concludes that the pace of everyday experiences now borders on mania. According to him, we have reached the heyday of speed. One of the defining characteristics of modern society is acceleration.

Peter Russell (1992) called the ever-increasing pace of modern life "acceleration syndrome." He noted that calculations that used to take decades are now made in minutes, that communication that used to take months now happens in seconds. He refers to the observations of the economist Georges Anderla who computed the rate at which the collective knowledge of the human family is accelerating. The collective knowledge held by the human family at A.D. 1 had taken approximately 50,000 years to develop. The knowledge then doubled by A.D. 1500, then again by 1750, then by 1900, then 1950, then 1960, then 1967, then 1973, the year of his study. Russell entitled his book *The White Hole in Time*, a play on "black hole in space." Just as the speed of objects being drawn into black holes accelerates exponentially as they near the black hole's horizon, the rate of change in the pace of modern life is increasing exponentially.

Everything seems to be getting faster. Whether it's downloading files from the Internet, preparing a microwave meal, or getting the oil changed on our car, we are constantly looking for ways to save a few seconds. It's often hard to know exactly what we are doing with all the time we are saving, except cramming more things into our schedules.

Technology itself has much to do with our "time famine." Social critic Jeremy Rifkin (1987), for example, suggested that what has changed is the very way in which we conceive of time. The incredible speeds at which computers operate, for example, are literally beyond human comprehension. Although you may be able to think about what a nanosecond is, you cannot experience it in any fashion. But once you become accustomed to the speed at which computers operate, other human activities seem incredibly slow. The resulting impatience can have negative consequences for your interactions with other people. For example, children used to the rapid pace and rich visual stimulation of computer games may have real difficulty switching gears to interact with friends and family who operate at a much slower pace or to attend carefully to what teachers are saying in their classrooms.

As we noted previously, one of the hottest areas for counselors in the 1980s was predicted to be leisure counseling, helping people find ways to spend their extra time. There was extensive speculation about changes in the extent of the workweek: Would it be thirty hours? Thirty-five hours? Certain occupations have always entailed long hours: owners of small businesses, top CEO's, medical residents. But increasingly, other occupations are joining this list. In corporations, the longer work hours gradually made their way from the highly compensated top executives, to middle management, to the administrative support staff and factory workers.

In addition, the hours spent on domestic chores, mainly by women, have not changed appreciably in the past several decades. Each "revolutionary" advance—the dishwasher, the laundry machine, the vacuum cleaner, and other modern appliances, brings with it higher expectations and standards of cleanliness. Whereas years ago basic cleanliness was an acceptable standard, today the standard is much higher. Of course, there's nothing inherently wrong with this, but as with the other topics we've covered, when is enough enough? At the turn of the last century, it would have been unheard of to wash a garment each time it is worn, and not only is that the standard today, but the garment must be springtime fresh, free of wrinkles, and the colors must be vibrant. Again, this is not a bad thing, but are we willing to accept that this means we may *never* see a reduction in our domestic chores?

There seem to be no easy antidotes to this predicament, for many of the "solutions" offered actually increase the pace of life. Popular media, such as *Time, Newsweek,* and business publications, have focused on this time squeeze and have offered advice on how to cram more productivity into each hour, or how to find time for brief getaways, which hopefully will make the craziness a little more tolerable. You often hear the expression, "There aren't enough hours in the day." No matter how lofty your station in life or how meager your possessions, you have exactly twenty-four hours to devote to your daily activities. Many people use the time squeeze as a convenient excuse to explain why they don't do various things, like, "I haven't got enough time to exercise," or "I don't have time to hunt for bargains," or "I don't have time to read the newspaper."

The truth is that every day you make decisions about how to spend your time. It's not that you don't have time for exercise, or for getting a physical examination, or for a lot of other important tasks, it is simply that you have chosen to fill your time with other activities. Of course, in the short term we all have various work and social obligations that have to be met—if you have agreed to take a sick relative to the doctor, you are not free to cancel that obligation because something else came up. Or if you have a small child, your day will be filled with numerous caretaking responsibilities. The same is true for jobs. But many of us manage to fill our days with endless lists of things to do, many of which are not vital to our interests. We refer to this needless pressure as the "tyranny of the trivia." If your constant focus is on the little things, you may ignore the big picture items that will ultimately determine your success and happiness. If you spend an inordinate amount of time with superficial relationships and obligations, you may be slighting deep, meaningful relationships. You may need to clarify your values and prioritize your time commitments accordingly.

If you feel that you don't have time to do the things you value, that is a clear indication that something in your lifestyle is out of kilter. Although you may not be able to change the way you allocate your time overnight, with enough planning and commitment, you can begin to make changes that invest you life with more meaning.

Consumerism and the Winner-Take-All Society

Barry Schwartz writes in his book *The Costs of Living* (1994) that our modern consumer-oriented society, despite its many benefits, has produced an "iron cage" for a great many people who are forced to spend almost all their time working for, and consuming, goods. Schwartz took the term "iron cage" from the following quote by economist Max Weber: "The care for external goods should only lie on the shoulders of the saint like a light cloak, which can be thrown aside at any moment. But fate decreed that the cloak should become an iron cage."

Despite the possession of material goods, many Americans feel more pressure today than ever before. It is not hard to see why. Billions of dollars are spent on advertising to flood you with images of products that you absolutely *must* have. Whether it's using the right mouthwash so your friends and family won't forsake you because of chronic halitosis, buying the right car so that you appear attractive to potential romantic partners, or turning your investments over to the right financial company so your children can go to college, you are literally bombarded with things you must buy.

Csikszentmihalyi (1999) points out that cross-national comparisons show a reasonable correlation between material and subjective well-being, but this relationship is far from perfect. Japan and Germany have more than twice the gross domestic product of Ireland, but report far lower levels of happiness. Studies in which wealthy individuals are compared to those with lesser financial resources show little difference in measures of reported happiness, even among those who acquire wealth suddenly, such as lottery winners

(Brickman, Coates, and Janoff-Bulman 1978). Both Csikszentmihalyi (1999) and Schwartz (1994) explain such findings by pointing out that humans have an annoying habit of quickly adjusting expectations for wealth as soon as it is accumulated. Numerous studies have confirmed that goals keep adjusting themselves upward as soon as lower levels are attained.

Another reason that material rewards do not necessarily make you happy is that when resources are unevenly distributed, people evaluate their possessions not in terms of what they need to live comfortably, but in comparison to those who have the most. Hundreds of years ago, the economics of societies were based on agriculture. People grew their own food and traded for what they could not produce themselves. Since there were very few commodities not possessed by the average person, there was little incentive to work harder than what was necessary to feed and clothe one's family. The Amish of Pennsylvania lead a similar lifestyle today, allowing material possessions to play a greatly diminished role in their value system.

The rapid proliferation of consumerism in this country seems to be accompanied by what economists Robert Frank and Phillip J. Cook (1995) see as the emergence of a "winner-take-all" society in which there is fierce competition for economic prizes that are fewer in number but greater in size. Arenas such as athletics, arts, and entertainment have always been structured this way. A precious few elite athletes, actors, and artists can earn staggering amounts of money, while the vast majority earn precious little. Frank and Cook point out that the influence of modern information and media has caused an increasing concentration of wealth and power in the hands of just a few.

However, being the top performer in a winner-take-all market may require being only slightly ahead of whoever is in second place. In athletics, running a few tenths or hundredths of a second faster than your competitors, being able to throw a football a little more accurately, or pitching a fastball a little harder can be the difference between getting cut from the team and earning millions of dollars. This means that competitors in a winner-take-all market must work extremely hard and sacrifice everything to make it to the top, because while margins of victory may be miniscule, the spoils go only to the victor.

Overcoming the Hazards of Modern Living

Despite Yeats's suggestion that you must choose work or personal happiness, many have suggested possible cures, or at least treatments, for our current predicament. Csikszentmihalyi (1999) suggests that the alternative to an addiction to material possessions has always been a spiritual approach. Today, we might also include the psychological approach. This approach is based on the premise that if happiness is a mental state, one should be able to control it through cognitive approaches. Although it is possible to control the mind through chemical means, Csikszentmihalyi points out that drugs lack an essential ingredient for producing sustained happiness: the knowledge that one is responsible for having achieved it. To this list, we might also add the risk of addiction, unlawful activities, and financial costs. Religions have also sought to provide followers with a subjective sense of well-being through teaching about rewards in the afterlife and the importance of good works on this earth. Many psychological methods also have been developed for "programming" the mind to increase happiness.

Csikszentmihalyi (1990) has made his own contribution in this area through his writings on the concept of *flow*, which describes a particular type of experience that is so engrossing and enjoyable that it becomes worth doing for its own sake, even though it may have no consequence outside itself. Artistic activities, sports, games, and religious activities are typical sources for such experiences, and some individuals seem capable of having them on a regular basis. Csikszentmihalyi described a number of common characteristics for such experiences. First, you must know clearly from moment to moment what you have to do, either because an activity requires it (such as the progression in which notes must be played for a given piece of music) or because you set clear goals for every step of the way (such as a mountain climber who must be intentional about every hand- and foothold). Second, you must be able to get immediate feedback on what you are doing, either because of the intrinsic nature of the activity (such as shooting free throws in basketball and knowing that you are hitting "nothing but net") or because you have an internalized set of standards that makes it possible to know whether you are meeting the standard (such as when a writer reviews what he has written and decides whether it needs revision).

A third element, which dovetails nicely with our discussion of the subjective nature of stress, is that you must feel that your abilities are adequate for the task at hand. If the challenges presented by the activity are too great, you are likely to feel anxious, and if your skills greatly exceed the requirements of the task, boredom is likely.

This description of flow underscores the idea that a subjective sense of well-being is not synonymous with material assets. Perhaps because of this, others have suggested that we attempt to scale back our wants and live within our means. Juliet Schor (1998) in *The Overspent*

American points out that many Americans are sinking into greater amounts of debt, in part because they have been sold a bills of goods (literally) about the connection between happiness and buying things.

This is most apparent during the holiday season, when you are encouraged to show your feelings for each other by spending as much as possible on gifts. You are inundated with such messages for weeks, and when the holidays are over and you have consumed all that you can, you are then barraged with ads for diet plans, exercise clubs, and consumer debt services. Schor suggests that one way to combat the work, earn, and spend cycle is for groups of individuals to act cooperatively to reduce their need to consume. For example, she suggests that neighborhoods set up cooperative arrangements whereby members share expensive equipment such as lawn tools that are infrequently used. Joe Dominguez and Vicki Robin (1993) suggest even more dramatic steps in *Your Money or Your Life*, a book that describes methods for getting off the frantic and addictive cycle of working, getting, and spending. Their book is a Zen-like translation of Benjamin Franklin's recommendations for frugality. They suggest that people start by totaling all of the money they have earned in their lifetime to get an idea of how rich and independent they might have become with a little more foresight and a little less impulse buying. Before every purchase, the authors suggest you ask yourself, "Is this what I want to exchange my life energy for?" In effect, they recommend a lifestyle of voluntary simplicity: for example, buying secondhand clothes, avoiding expensive dining out, canceling magazine and cable subscriptions, and taking lunch to work.

Our point in this chapter is not that the American dream is a sham or that technology represents a curse to humanity. But as we will detail throughout this book, perhaps the single most important factor in controlling stress is having a sense of control over your life. And at times, modern living can leave you with a sense that you are not in control of your life. Some people even feel that they are simply an extension of the many machines and technologies that surround them. You may feel caught on a treadmill of work and spend. It is no wonder that many individuals feel worried, tense, and confused much of the time. But our message here is one of hope, not of despair. As Andrew Shapiro (1999) argues in *The Control Revolution*, new technologies such as the personal computer and the Internet can give you more control over information, resources, and your experiences than ever before if you understand and use them properly. You have many options for taming technologies and many avenues available in daily life for moderating your wants and your stress. Throughout the following chapters, we offer many suggestions for doing so.

Chapter 3

Road Map for Understanding Stress

One thing is sure. We have to do something. We have to do the best we know how at the moment. If it doesn't turn out right, we can modify it as we go along.

—Franklin D. Roosevelt

Imagine trying to drive across the continent with only a compass for direction. You know where you want to go, but you have no road maps to guide you. Certainly, the route would be roundabout and frustrating. You would probably take many wrong turns along the way, expend a great deal of wasted effort, and probably experience more than your share of discomfort. In a similar fashion, many efforts at coping with stressful situations are misguided. Without a proper understanding of stress, our efforts to cope may fail badly. At times, what we do to cope with stress may actually create *more* stress and *more* pain. Surely a road map for dealing with stress is essential. This chapter offers a map for understanding stress and Chapter 5 presents a road map for understanding coping. These maps will become important guides for your understanding and actions when facing stressful events, and we will return to them many times in subsequent chapters.

The Construction of the Stress Road Map

As we noted in the last chapter, early stress researchers were primarily concerned with either stressful events or the physical changes your body undergoes when dealing with such events. Thomas Holmes and Richard Rahe focused attention on the importance of external events by constructing the Social Readjustment Rating Scale to measure them (Holmes and Rahe 1967), and Hans Selye (1956) contributed greatly to our understanding of the physiological changes constituting the stress response. Our current understanding of the stress process is more comprehensive.

Contemporary researchers see stress as the result of a transaction between the person and the environment. According to these

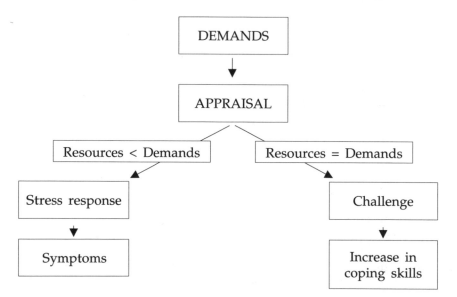

Figure 3-1. Road Map for Understanding Stress

researchers, stress is not something that happens to you. Rather, it is the result of the *meaning* you assign to events that happen to you. Consequently, the notion of *appraisal* is assigned a major role in explanations of the stress process. It is your appraisal of the seriousness of the event and the adequacy of your coping resources that determines whether you will respond stressfully. Figure 3-1 presents a road map for understanding stress.

The Many-Faceted Nature of Demands

Notice that at the top of Figure 3-1 that the stress process is begun when you encounter a *demand*. Demands are requirements placed on you. They may be self-imposed or they may come from role requirements, life changes, or daily hassles. A demand may be something as minor as an irritating call from a telephone solicitor or as major as a fire in your apartment building. Keep in mind that at this point, we are not calling the demand a stressor, because not every demand ends up becoming a stressor.

Perhaps the most frequent and exacting demands are *self-requirements*. They may include perfectionist expectations such as requiring yourself to be a "straight A" student, to make a million dollars by the time you are thirty-five years old, or to be the most popular person at school or work. The list of self-demands may go on and on, and often people have little tolerance for failing to meet them.

Many demands for coping come from the *roles* you play. These requirements stem from your status as a family member, spouse, romantic partner, employee, parent, student, or community member. As opposed to self-requirements, role requirements come from other people and are less under your control. Obligations stemming from role requirements can occur suddenly and unexpectedly, such as the need to care for a sick child, spouse, or family member. A third type of demand is significant *life changes,* such as getting married or divorced, starting school or a new job, moving to a new home, contracting a serious illness, or experiencing a financial crisis. The clustering of life change events may overwhelm your coping resources and contribute to performance failures and health problems.

As we have mentioned, there is strong evidence that a fourth type of stressor, *daily hassles,* can be even more detrimental to your health than major events (Kanner, Coyne, Schaefer, and Lazarus 1981). Daily hassles can include a wide range of relatively minor events that plague everyday life: appliances that break down, traffic snarls, sales clerks with attitudes, or an unexpected downpour. Hassles may threaten your happiness even more than major events because they are so common that you may be embarrassed to ask for help from others in coping with them. Although a major life change such as losing your job can have far-ranging negative consequences, you are also more likely to receive support from others in coping with.

It's important to remember that demands are subject to individual interpretations. Not all demands will affect people the same way. For instance, many students meet the end of the school year with great excitement, but others are disappointed to see it end. And the breakup of a romantic relationship may seem like the end of the world for the person getting "dumped," but may be a relief to the person who breaks it off. The difference of course lies in how you interpret the event, a process we have already referred to as cognitive appraisal.

Appraising Demands and Resources

Now take a moment to look back at Figure 3-1. Notice that in this road map awareness of a demand is followed by our appraisals of the situation. When confronted with a potentially stressful situation, you typically suspend action while you attempt to get a better reading on the demand. *Appraisal* is a word used in the business world when one is estimating the value of a piece of property. When used by stress researchers, however, it refers to the subjective evaluations you make about life demands. The impact of a stressful event is a function not only of the properties of the event itself, but also of the appraisal you make of your ability to cope with it.

Primary and Secondary Appraisal

The appraisal process, therefore, actually involves two substeps. The first substep, primary appraisal, involves an evaluation of the significance of the event itself. In effect, you ask yourself the question, "Am I in trouble?" This mental step has a strong influence on your daily well-being. If you consistently register threats in your environment, you are going to spend a great deal of time being stressed out.

Consider those forced into Nazi death camps during World War II. Prisoners in places such as Auschwitz literally feared for their lives every moment of the day. When they asked themselves, "Am I in trouble?" the answer was always yes. Even worse was that the exact nature and timing of the threat was unknown—some were allowed to live on in the death camps until the end of the war, while others were put to death immediately.

In some cases, primary appraisals can occur quite rapidly or be bypassed altogether. We would not have survived very long as a species if, when encountering a bear or snake in the wilderness, we spent precious seconds pondering whether or not that creature posed a threat to us. Consider the case of phobias: When encountering a spider, a dog, or high elevations, some individuals immediately experience the stress response without any deliberation. Such stimuli are automatic triggers for the stress response, and phobic individuals will go to just about any length to avoid them.

After making a primary appraisal about a given demand and asking yourself, "What's at stake here?" you then ask yourself the next logical question, "Can I handle it?" This secondary appraisal is based on what you perceive to be your capacity for handling life demands. We will provide a way for you to inventory some of these capacities in chapter 6. But first, we hope to make clear the distinction between primary and secondary appraisals.

Primary vs. Secondary Appraisals

Following are two different examples of self-statements from a hypothetical situation in which Tom and Jane get a flat tire. Read the examples below and then take a moment to consider the types of primary and secondary appraisals being made in each example.

Example 1

Demand	*Tom's Self-statement*
Flat tire while driving	"Oh my God! There's something wrong with the car. It's a hundred degrees out and I'm miles from a telephone. What will I do?"

What type of primary appraisal is Tom making about getting a flat tire, and what type of secondary appraisal is he making about the sufficiency of his resources for coping with it? Write your best guess about what Tom is telling himself about the event in the space below:

Example 1: Tom's primary appraisal _____

Next, what is Tom likely telling himself about his capacity for handling this event? Please write your answer in the space below:

Example 1: Secondary appraisal _____

Now, let's turn to example two, in which Jane experiences the same event.

Example 2

Demand	*Jane's Self-statement*
Flat tire while driving	"Uh oh, another flat. Guess I'll have to change it. I'd better get the spare out of the trunk."

Obviously, based on the self-statement provided above, Jane is having a very different reaction to getting a flat tire! Again, think about Jane's primary appraisal and write it in the space below:

Example 2: Primary appraisal _____

Next, please think about what type of secondary appraisal Jane is making in example 2, and write it in the space below:

Example 2: Secondary appraisal _____

Now for the answers. We hope it's obvious that in Jane's case (example 2), she views the flat tire as an inconvenience but not as a life-or-death matter. She is appraising the situation as significant enough to warrant immediate attention but not likely to involve imminent bodily harm. As a result of this primary appraisal, Jane is likely telling herself something like, "This flat tire is a pain, but it's not that big a deal." As for secondary appraisal of her coping resources, Jane has obviously concluded her resources are sufficient to tackle the problem, perhaps saying to herself, "Well, I haven't done this in a while, but I can handle it. I'd better get the spare out of the trunk."

However, even though it's the same event, you see a much different picture in Tom's case (example 1). He seems to view the flat tire as one step short of Armageddon, and given the nature of the catastrophe, it's no wonder he has concluded his resources are insufficient. Therefore, his primary appraisal is probably something like, "This is just about the worse thing that could happen to me right now!" and his secondary appraisal may be along the line of, "There's no way I'm going to be able to handle this without major assistance." It's easy to imagine Jane rolling up her sleeves and getting to work right away fixing the flat tire. It's also easy to imagine Tom ranting and raving on the side of the road while other motorists whiz by.

We hope this example illustrates the subjective nature of stress. Ultimately, we hope to show that you have the potential to exercise considerable control over the appraisals you make. It all begins with your primary appraisal about what's at stake when encountering a demand. Many people shoot themselves in the foot (psychologically speaking) from the beginning by making inaccurate primary appraisals of life demands.

How Demands Trigger the Stress Response

Your appraisals of any given life demand will lead you to one of three possible conclusions:

1. You may conclude that the demand is irrelevant; that is, that it likely involves no significant consequence for you—in which case you simply may ignore it.

2. You may conclude that it constitutes a reasonable challenge to your resources and thereby offers you an opportunity to practice your coping skills. A challenge may be thought of as involving an optimal amount of stimulation. People who are optimally challenged are able to lose themselves in tasks and their efforts do not seem like work. Whereas chronic stress may drain your resources and lower immune efficiency, successfully coping with challenges often enriches your coping resources and strengthens your immune system.

3. Finally, you may conclude that it exceeds your resources for dealing with it and may signal harm, threat, or loss.

In this third case, where you conclude that your resources are inadequate for the demand, you will experience the stress response to some degree. The intensity of the stress response will depend on how serious you believe the consequences will be if you fail to cope adequately. Thus, you might confront a demand that exceeds your resources and yet experience very little stress—if you were to conclude that succeeding or failing doesn't make much difference to you anyway. Here is yet another way that your interpretations, your appraisals, influence the amount of stress you experience.

It is important to recognize the pivotal role your appraisals play in creating stress. As Shakespeare wrote in *Hamlet*, "There is nothing either good or bad, but thinking makes it so." Appraisals create something of a fork in the road when it comes to stress: If you appraise demands as outstripping your resources (Rewards < Demands in Figure 3-1), you will likely experience the stress response with its many attendant stress symptoms. But if you see yourself as up to the task (Rewards = Demands in Figure 3-1), you experience challenge and the opportunity to increase your capacities for coping. In some ways handling stress can be a feast or famine situation. If you cope successfully with demands, you become energized and invigorated. If not, you stand to lose your physical, emotional, and spiritual health.

Benefits of Successful Coping

You can't completely eliminate stress from daily life, nor would you want to. Many science-fiction authors, such as Aldous Huxley in *Brave New World* or George Orwell in *1984,* have written cautionary tales about future worlds where science or the government has completely taken over the lives of citizens, rendering everyday existence lifeless and inert. Much of the meaning that we derive from life comes from the fact that we are constantly challenged by a world that is always changing and evolving. We are problem-solving beings. We mostly *like* challenges. They offer us an opportunity to flex our coping muscles, often strengthening them and increasing our repertoire of skills and resources. The energized feeling we get from successful coping even has a name of its own: *eustress.* But remember, a challenge is a demand that you feel *up* for. If you conclude that your resources for coping with the demand are inadequate, your appraisal triggers a stress response. The key to successful coping, therefore, lies in the ability to balance perceived demands with perceived resources for coping, thereby keeping the level of arousal within an optimal range.

The Stress Response

The stress response, you will recall from chapter 1, is nature's way of preparing you to fight tigers—real ones or metaphorical ones, the physiological changes are the same. If an attack on your life were imminent, your body would undergo numerous changes to prepare for combat. The pupils of the eyes would dilate to increase your peripheral vision to better detect blows from the right or left. Because considerable energy would be required, your breathing would deepen to increase your oxygen supply, and your liver would begin to increase your blood sugar. Your heartbeat would speed up to circulate the blood, now engorged with oxygen and blood sugar, to the muscles in the arms and legs and to the brain. Your kidneys would produce a substance to cause constriction of the vessels, and the pituitary and adrenal glands would cause the body to retain more fluids. The excess fluids would filter into the circulation system to increase your blood volume. The combined action of increased heart rate, the narrowing of the arteries, and the increased blood volume would significantly elevate your blood pressure. It is not surprising, then, that stress is recognized as a major contributor to hypertension.

Under stress, the muscles of the body contract sharply for battle. If a predatory animal attacked you, you would want your muscles to be highly toned to run or fight. If muscles, however, remain tense for long periods, they may pinch nerves running within the muscles, creating tension headaches and backaches. Moreover, the sharp contraction of muscles will decrease the blood supply by pinching arterioles, venuoles, and capillaries. One of the functions of the circulatory system is to serve as trash collector, to pick up poorly burned fuel, called metabolites, and to return them to be burned again as fuel. If the overly contracted muscles decrease the efficiency of the circulatory system, the metabolites may build up. Certain metabolites, such as lactic acid, fatigue muscle tissue. Consequently, highly stressed individuals may experience so much tiredness that they suspect they are suffering from chronic fatigue syndrome.

Stress Symptoms

Refer again to Figure 3-1. Once the stress response has been triggered, sustained periods of stress arousal can result in symptoms that deteriorate the quality of your life and imperil your health. There are four categories of these symptoms: symptoms that affect cognitive processes, emotions, behavior, and health.

Cognitive symptoms

The stress response prepares you for quick action, not clear thinking. If a predatory animal confronted you, it would not be necessary to become creative—simply running or fighting would do. During such episodes, action is favored over cognition. Consequently, your attention, concentration, and memory suffer badly at such times. Others talk but you're not listening, because your attention is locked in on your problems. You are so aroused that you have trouble sustaining concentration on complex tasks. You have difficulty making use of your past experience, because your memories serve you poorly at such times. This cognitive impairment is doubly disappointing, because most modern stressors require creative solutions. You often are asked to juggle multiple tasks, to prioritize them, and to clarify sticky issues. All of these functions are performed less efficiently under heavy stress.

Emotional Symptoms

Feelings of anger, irritation, fear, anxiety, and depression are the most frequent outcomes of the stress response. Under stress you may become irritable and verbally lash out at those around you. Or worse yet, persistent, unresolved problems may dam up your anger until it becomes a burning rage that floods your body with strong stress hormones. The threatening nature of many stressors creates anxious states. When the stressors are pervasive and poorly understood, you may experience a kind of generalized anxiety—vague feelings of uncertainty and danger that are more or less constant. Additionally, chronic bouts with stressors contribute markedly to situational depression by depleting certain biochemicals that stimulate reward centers of the brain.

Behavioral Symptoms

The body's stress hormones empower the muscles for physical effort, but this can interfere with your ability to function effectively. Several years ago a two-year-old infant escaped his mother's watchful eye and ventured into the street, where he was run over by a pickup truck. The driver abruptly stopped the vehicle when he realized he had hit the child. The mother heard the screech of the truck's tires, ran into the street, and found to her horror that one of the rear tires rested on the abdomen of the child. She yelled and gestured at the driver, urging him to move the truck off her son, but the driver was frozen from fear. Empowered by her stress hormones, this 117-pound mother literally lifted the rear of the truck and freed her son! Although the stress response may power the large muscles for gross reactions, it can also interfere with intricate maneuvers such as performing surgery, shooting at a target, or even threading a needle.

Stress often incites restlessness and interferes with sleep. Some sleep scientists claim that America has a greater sleep debt than national debt. Most people fail to appreciate the critical influence of sleep upon performance and a sense of well-being. Without proper sleep your decision-making capacity is sorely impaired, seriously undermining your ability to function effectively. Many major tragedies have resulted from decisions made during periods of sleeplessness. Notable examples are the Bhopal chemical factory explosion, the nuclear meltdown at Chernobyl, the Challenger explosion, and the Exxon *Valdez* oil spill (Wyatt 2000). The National Transportation Safety Board concluded that sleep deprivation was the direct cause of the Exxon *Valdez* oil spill. The third mate who was left on the bridge to steer the ship through the ice floes had slept only six hours in the previous forty-eight and was severely sleep deprived. The Human Factors Subcommittee of the Rogers Commission concluded that the decision to launch the Challenger was an error on the part of NASA managers who were severely sleep deprived at the time (Dement and Vaughn 1999). Sleep deficits also will impair memory consolidation, the repair of worn-out body tissue, and your sense of temporal and spatial orientation. We will discuss the importance of sleep further in chapter 6.

Health Symptoms

Prolonged periods of stress may interfere with your natural defenses against infectious diseases and cancer. Two classes of stress biochemicals, catacholamines and corticoids, are both known to interfere with immune functioning. These stress biochemicals increase the concentration of free fatty acids (cholesterol and trigylcerides), elevate the blood pressure and contribute to atherosclerosis, coronary heart disease, and stroke. Stress also aggravates medical conditions such as diabetes mellitus, rheumatoid arthritis, systemic lupus erythmatosus, and allergies. The hurtful effects of stress on health are complex and pervasive.

Combat or Détente? Two Forms of Coping

Figure 3-1 suggests that demands appraised as exceeding your resources trigger the stress response, resulting in the myriad stress symptoms just described. But we know the process doesn't end there—in one form or another, you respond to such events by undertaking some form of coping. We have alluded to the importance of coping in handling stress, but it's now time to get a little more specific about the various ways individuals can cope. In general, coping refers to efforts to eliminate or alter stressors or to control your emotional response to them. An attack on the stressor is referred to as *problem-focused* coping, and an effort to control one's emotional response to the stressor is referred to as *emotion-focused* coping (Folkman and Lazarus 1980). Problem-focused forms of coping typically are more appropriate when the stressor is appraised as being changeable or controllable, whereas emotion-focused forms of coping are more appropriate when the stressor is believed to be uncontrollable. Figure 3-2 picks up where Figure 3-1 left off, depicting the relationship between the two forms of coping that occur after you become stressed.

In reality, you generally use a mixture of problem-focused and emotion-focused coping. Sometimes one form of coping may facilitate the other. There are times when emotion-focused coping is needed to succeed in attacking the stressor. For example, you may need to use emotion-focused coping to reduce your anxiety so you can successfully make a public presentation. In other cases, problem-focused coping may remove the need for emotion-focused coping. For example, thrusting yourself into your work and completing a job may have an anxiety-reducing, emotion-focused effect.

With regard to any specific demand, these various forms of coping may be effective or ineffective, helpful or hurtful. The

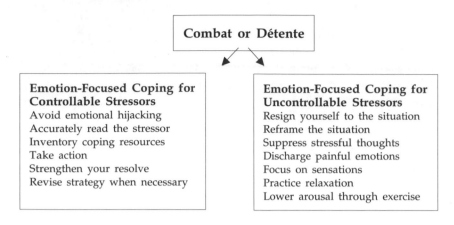

Figure 3-2. Two-dimensional model for coping.

effectiveness of coping depends upon the accuracy of the appraisal of demands and resources and the appropriateness of the coping strategy chosen. Coping may be ineffective if the situation is misread. Misreading a potentially harmful situation means that necessary anticipatory coping may not take place. On the other hand, appraising a benign situation as threatening may lead to wasteful coping efforts. The effectiveness of your coping also will depend on the choice of a coping strategy. In dealing with stressors, it is important to know whether to combat them or to declare détente. The well-known prayer of Saint Francis of Assisi clearly states the options:

> Give me the strength to accept with serenity the things that cannot be changed.
> Give me the courage to change the things that can and should be changed.
> And give me the wisdom to distinguish one from the other.

The kicker in the prayer is the last line—"And give me the wisdom to distinguish one from the other." It's often confusing to know whether there *is* any reasonable action to take. Personality differences, for example, can influence your judgment at such times. Reticent, fearful people are more likely to underestimate the possibilities for eliminating the stressor, whereas more confident, "can-do" people may attack even when détente would be more appropriate.

We will look at this issue more closely in chapter 5. But first we'll use the map for understanding how stress is triggered to look at methods for identifying and negotiating specific life demands.

Chapter 4

Negotiating Demands

Anything that can go wrong, will go wrong.

—Murphy's Law

Most people think dramatically, not quantitatively.

—Oliver Wendell Holmes,
late Supreme Court Justice

If you have ever tossed and turned in the wee hours of the morning because of an impending exam, job interview, or doctor visit, and then caught a glimpse of your pet stretched out at the foot of the bed snoozing away without a care in the world, you might have been struck by the fact that animals spend very little time worrying about the future. Your dog or cat isn't going to spend one second worrying about death unless it's staring it in the face; in fact, dogs and cats probably can't even conceive of their own mortality. In darker moments, we may suspect that they are better off for not being "afflicted" with self-awareness. They do what they do, day after day, and don't waste time or energy wondering whether they should be doing it or not. This is perhaps one reason that we keep pets in the first place: We get a little perspective from them.

While we might fantasize about it at times, few of us would volunteer to change places with our pets by trading our intellectual abilities for the "bliss" of ignorance. Contemplating future is the main reason we are not out in the wilderness with the rest of the animal kingdom, freezing in the cold or getting soaked in the rain. Over the past several thousand years, human beings have gained more and more control over the outside world because of their ability to anticipate, understand, and plan for things that haven't yet happened.

But as we have already suggested, our ability to forecast the future is far from perfect. Unfortunately, nature seems to prefer that we overreact to a hundred phantom demands rather than be blindsided by a single unforeseen threat. What was once a formula for survival in the wilderness is a recipe for lifelong misery today

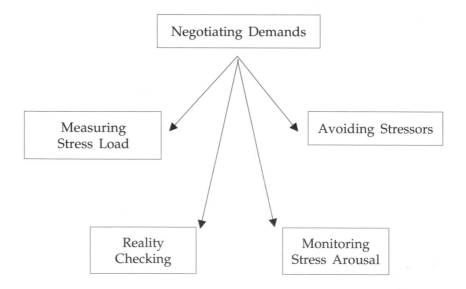

Figure 4-1.   Negotiating demands.

unless we can recalibrate our "stress sensors" and make wise decisions about which demands pose actual, rather than perceived, threats.

Here we'll discuss four specific methods for negotiating life demands: 1) measuring the demands you are facing; 2) checking the accuracy of your perceptions of these demands; 3) monitoring levels of stress arousal caused by demands; and 4) avoiding stressors whenever possible. Each of these four components of negotiating demands is illustrated in Figure 4-1 above.

The idea of this fourfold approach is that you should be very selective about which demands you allow yourself to treat as stressors. Learning to properly evaluate demands is in some ways even more important than learning methods to cope with stress. We present this informatin first, because, after working your way through the material in this chapter, you might find that many of your current demands are *not worth your coping efforts*. Once you have decided that a given demand is in fact a stressor, it will still take a toll, *even if you handle it successfully*. Therefore, the ideal method for coping with stress is to head off demands whenever possible *before* they become stressful, thus conserving resources for more pressing needs.

Measuring Your Stress Load

The clustering of multiple demands in a short period may temporarily exhaust your resources and trigger emotional and physical problems. It's important to pick your battles, to adjust the demand load, and to conserve your resources for coping. The effectiveness of your efforts to do so will depend, of course, on your accuracy in appraising demands and resources. To assist you in assessing your stress load, we are including an assessment instrument called the Social Readjustment Rating Scale (SRRS).

The SRRS lists forty-three life events that require adaptative behaviors, along with an index of the seriousness of these events. The authors, Drs. Thomas Holmes and Richard Rahe, maintain that one's ability to resist illness diminishes with the clustering of life events, and research has tended to confirm their assumption (Wyler, Masuda, and Holmes 1971). Age seems to play a role in the number and types of demands that individuals encounter. For example, younger people typically experience more of the life changes on the SRRS and older people fewer. We will return to the relationship of one's age to demands shortly. But first, take a few minutes to assess your stress load.

Social Readjustment Rating Scale (SRRS)
(Life Change Scale)

Instructions: Check each life event you have experienced over the past twelve months. If the event happened more than once, check it for each time up to a maximum of four times. Multiply the Life Change Unit value (LCU) of the event by the number of times you checked it and record the value in the "Your Score" column. Total these values at the bottom of the list to get your overall LCU score.

Life Event	Number	Value	Score
1. Death of a spouse	___	100	___
2. Divorce	___	73	___
3. Marital separation	___	65	___
4. Jail term	___	63	___
5. Death of a close family member	___	63	___
6. Major personal injury or illness	___	53	___
7. Marriage	___	50	___
8. Fired from work	___	47	___
9. Marital reconciliation	___	45	___
10. Retirement	___	45	___
11. Change in the health of family member	___	44	___
12. Pregnancy	___	40	___
13. Sexual difficulties	___	39	___
14. Gaining a new family member (e.g., through birth, adoption, older person moving in)	___	39	___
15. Business readjustment (e.g., merger, reorganization, bankruptcy)	___	39	___
16. Change in financial state (e.g., a lot worse off or a lot better off than usual)	___	38	___
17. Death of a close friend	___	37	___
18. Change to different line of work	___	36	___
19. Change in the number of arguments with spouse	___	35	___
20. Mortgage or loan for a major purpose (e.g., purchasing a home or business)	___	31	___
21. Foreclosure on mortgage or loan	___	30	___

22. Change in responsibilities at work (e.g., promotion, demotion, lateral transfer) ____   29   ____
23. Son or daughter leaving home (e.g., marriage, attending college) ____   29   ____
24. Trouble with in-laws ____   29   ____
25. Outstanding personal achievement ____   28   ____
26. Wife begins or stops work ____   26   ____
27. Begin or end school ____   26   ____
28. Change in living conditions (e.g., building a new home, remodeling, deterioration of home or neighborhood) ____   25   ____
29. A revision of personal habits (e.g., dress, manners, associations) ____   24   ____
30. Trouble with the boss ____   23   ____
31. Change in working hours or conditions ____   20   ____
32. Change in residence ____   20   ____
33. Changing schools ____   20   ____
34. Change in recreation ____   19   ____
35. A major change in church activities ____   19   ____
36. Change in social activities (e.g., clubs, dancing, movies, visiting) ____   18   ____
37. Taking out a mortgage or loan for a lesser purchase (e.g., for a car, TV, freezer) ____   17   ____
38. Change in sleeping habits (e.g., a lot more or lot less sleep, or change in part of day when asleep) ____   16   ____
39. Change in number of family get-togethers ____   15   ____
40. Change in eating habits (e.g., a lot more or a lot less food intake, or very different meal hours or surroundings) ____   15   ____
41. Vacation ____   13   ____
42. Christmas ____   12   ____
43. Minor violations of the law (e.g., traffic tickets, jaywalking, disturbing the peace) ____   11   ____

Total Life Change Score ____

Source: Reprinted from T. H. Holmes and R. H. Rahe, "The Social Readjustment Rating Scale," *Journal of Psychosomatic Research, 11,* (1967), 213–218. Copyright © 1967, with permission of Elseview Science.

The Scoring Key for the SRRS

Multiply the value of each event you experienced by the number of times it happened. Then add LCU scores for each event and record the figure in the "Total Life Change Score" space at the end of the list.

So what does your score mean? This scale has been retested with thousands of subjects in the United States, Belgium, Holland, France, and Japan. In each nation the results seem to indicate that too much life change over a short period initiates illness, and the greater the number of life changes, the more serious the illness. If your score falls between 0 and 149, you are said to have a 30 percent chance of experiencing an illness in the near future. A score of 150–299 earns you a 50 percent chance, and a score of 300 or higher, an 80 percent chance (Amundson, Hart, and Holmes 1981). But we're not done estimating your stress level yet! As we've noted, perceptions about the nature of demands matter a great deal.

The Importance of Perception

In constructing the Social Readjustment Rating Scale, the authors assumed that these life events would have the same effect on all people. The authors of the SRRS maintained that both negative *and* positive life events would increase one's vulnerability to future illness. However, Brown and McGill (1988) found that positive life events were detrimental to one's health only among people with negative self-views. Positive events seemed to *lessen* the incidence of illness among persons with high self-esteem and to *increase* the incidence among those with low self-esteem. Such research strongly suggests that the relationship of life events to stress and illness will be modified by factors within the person—factors such as self-esteem and the perception of control.

Research conducted by one of the authors (Matheny and Cupp 1983) suggests that taking into consideration the person's *perceptions* of these events strengthens the relationship between scores on the SRRS and illness. If at the time life events were being experienced, the person had perceived them as desirable, they were less predictive of future illness. Similarly, if people had anticipated and prepared for such life events beforehand, they were less predictive of future illness. Just as stepping off a curb without knowing it is there is shocking, major life changes that blindside you will prove particularly stressful. The perception of *control*, however, had the greatest moderating effect. Scoring only the SRRS events over which the person felt *no control* increased the value of the score in predicting future illness by roughly 400 percent! Life events over which persons *did feel* control were entirely *un*related to future illness. Consequently, your score on the SRRS will be a better indicator of your vulnerability to future illness if you take control into consideration.

Ask yourself, "Did I feel control over the event at the time I was experiencing it?" If "yes," eliminate the LCU value from your score; *then* apply the above scoring key.

Revised Life Change Score: _____

People today seem to view the SRRS life events more seriously than they did when the scale was first published in 1965. Mark Miller and Richard Rahe (1997) found that on average the ratings assigned these events in 1995 were 45 percent higher than in 1965! Perhaps the dizzying pace of modern living has reduced our reservoir of energy for dealing with life changes. There were also significant gender differences in the ratings. Overall women rated events 17 percent higher than men. Miller and Rahe concluded that this difference in rating is more a result of men under-reacting to life stress than women over-reacting. Previous research had shown that men who had experienced heart attacks tended to deny very severe symptoms in their illness. Moreover, women began remedial action once they were told their life stresses were high and their coping resources were low. Men did so, however, only after receiving lifestyle counseling and repeated encouragement to do so.

Hassles Can Also Be Demanding

As we noted in previous chapters, Richard Lazarus and his colleagues have suggested a distinction between major life events and everyday hassles. In the short term, hassles may have an even greater effect on wellness than major life events, because they occur continuously (Kanner, Coyne, Schaefer, and Lazarus 1981). In one study, Lazarus (1981) asked 100 white, middle-class, middle-aged men and women to keep track of their hassles for one year. The following hassles were the ten most common:

1. Concern about weight

2. Health of a family member

3. Rising prices of consumer goods

4. Home maintenance

5. Too many things to do

6. Misplacing or losing things

7. Yard work

8. Property, investment, or taxes

9. Crime

10. Physical appearance

This list of hassles suggest that the SRRS checklist we presented earlier is probably only a beginning step in getting a complete reading on demands. It's important to consider the many hassles that pop up in everyday life, especially those that occur on a consistent basis (for example, getting stuck in rush-hour traffic). There always will be hassling experiences of one sort or another. If we are to limit the emotional costs of dealing with these hassling events, we must accept them as a part of the dues we pay for membership in the human family. Accepting them and patiently dealing with them is the most cost-effective approach.

Whether or not demands come in the form of minor hassles or major events, the exact nature of the stress you experience can also vary widely with age. Therefore, the following section addresses relatively unique demands that tend to cluster at the beginning and the end of the life span.

A Developmental View of Demands

The list of demands included in the SRRS are *most* relevant to individuals in middle adulthood—i.e., those who have finished school, are working, and have one or more family members living with them. People who are either younger or much older than middle adulthood may face unique challenges.

First, let's examine the demands that today's youngsters face. Although it is widely recognized that adults can experience harmful levels of stress in dealing with everyday demands, this awareness does not yet appear to extend to children and adolescents. A survey conducted by *USA Today* asked adults what age they'd like to remain for the rest of their lives if they could. Only 12 percent of the men and 16 percent of the women polled chose any age less than fifteen (*USA Today*, 1998). However, many adults still subscribe to the myth that the lot of children is idyllic—that their problems are inconsequential when compared to the weighty problems of adults. This misperception may stem in part from viewing childhood problems through the lens of adult coping resources. In all likelihood, children experience far less control than adults because many of their choices are made for them, choices including where they will live, what they will eat, and how they will spend most of their day. However, parent ratings of the seriousness of stressors in the lives of their children are at best only moderately related to the ratings of their children. Consequently, stress has the potential to exact an exorbitant toll from children and adolescents that can often go unrecognized by the adults responsible for them.

We recently conducted a survey of the types of stressors that 1,500 middle school children face in south-central Texas (McCarthy, Seraphine, Matheny, and Curlette 2000). These students represented a wide range of ethnic backgrounds and socioeconomic levels, as well as equal numbers of girls and boys. The top ten stressors cited by these youngsters are listed below, as well as the percentage who responded "yes" to each item.

Stressors	*Percentage responding yes*
1. A lot of students in my school have fights.	56%
2. Not living with both parents	48%
3. Can't talk to teachers	34.1%
4. Moved within the last year	33.4%
5. Other students take my belongings	31.5%
6. Afraid to ask teacher questions in class	31.4%
7. Feel like I lose at sports or games often	28%
8. Have a great deal of crime in my neighborhood	25%
9. Have scary dreams	24.5%
10. Classroom is too crowded	24.3%

This list of stressors for children may surprise the average adult. Adjustment to school and fear of violence are the two major themes running through this list. Children need the support and understanding of parents and teachers in dealing with these issues. Bolstering their sense of personal adequacy would help them feel more comfortable in the school setting. Attempts to counter the excessive attention given to crime and violence by the media would add to their sense of security.

Stress in Older People

Unique demands also occur at the other end of the life span. Among the first European settlers in America the average life span was approximately thirty-three years; by 1900 it had advanced to forty-seven, and then to seventy-six years in 1999 (Weiner 1999). In other words, the age composition of the American population has changed radically over the years. As late as 1790, when the first census was taken, one half of the population was under sixteen years of age. Currently, less than 25 percent of the population is under sixteen, and the Census Bureau projects that Americans over sixty-five will outnumber teenagers two to one by the year 2025.

Robert Sapolsky defines aging as "the progressive loss of the ability to deal with stress (1998, p. 199)." As we suggested previously, middle-aged individuals may experience more episodic daily hassles involving work, finance, family, and friends, but older adults may experience more daily hassles dealing with the environment, social issues, home maintenance, and chronic health problems. In addition, stress may be more costly to older adults, because their neurophysiological systems are not as efficient in handling it. Stress may also contribute to the aging process, and the aging process in turn creates additional stress.

There is some evidence, however, that in spite of eroding capacities, multiple losses, and increasing illnesses, the oldest of the old report that they are happier, experience fewer stressful events, and have fewer negative emotions than young and middle-aged adults (Mroczek and Kolarz 1998). Studies of the "oldest old," those more than eighty-five years old, suggest that conscientiousness (achievement striving, competence, and deliberation) and stable interpersonal ties predict longevity (Friedman et al 1975); that their ability to modulate their emotions appears to facilitate their adjustment to stressors (Johnson 1998); and that their low neuroticism scores suggest that they felt "secure, hardy, and generally relaxed even under stressful conditions" (Silver, Bubrick, Jilinskaia, and Perls 1998). The New England Centenarian Study concluded that female centenarians (there were too few males in the sample to allow for conclusions) are particularly good at managing stress. It also seems that older people may appraise stressors differently than younger people. They seem to sense their dwindling energy and try to conserve it by disclaiming responsibility for many problems, viewing them as either inevitable or irrelevant (Aldwin 1994). They seem to be saving their energy for more important battles.

In his research, one of the authors of this book examined the published literature to identify recommended coping strategies for older adults addressing the ten most undesirable events for each gender as reported on the Louisville Older Person Events Scale (LOPES) (Matheny et al. 2000). Interestingly, while the first seven stressors were the same for both genders, the bottom three were not. The findings are presented in the table below.

Thirteen Most Undesirable Events
Experienced by Older Adults

Events for Both Genders

1. Spouse died

2. Child died

3. Grandchild died

4. Lost home

5. Sibling died

6. Separation because of conflict

7. Experienced new illness or injury

Additional Events for Females

8. Parent died

9. Spouse had new illness or injury

10. Child had new illness or injury

Additional Events For Males:

8. New problem in marriage

9. Parent had new illness or injury

10. Lost job or business

Both children and older adults experience special difficulties in coping with stressors unique to their age groups. Children lack an experiential base that would help them to place their problems in a more accurate perspective, and compared to adults, their coping resources are underdeveloped. Older people have their special problems in coping as well. They are dealing with a dwindling supply of energy, and their bodies are sustaining greater damage from stress biochemicals. The baseline levels of certain stress biochemicals are greater in older people and once the stress response has increased the production of these biochemicals, they return to their baseline levels more slowly. The higher concentrations of these biochemicals may lead to depression and lowered immune functioning. Although stressors may be more costly to older people, their greater life experiences may help them to achieve a less stressful perspective on the normal demands of living.

Reality Checking: Are Demands Real or Imagined?

With no shortage of things to worry about, we can easily become paralyzed with fear, unable to sort out the real risks from the exaggerated ones. H. Aaron Cohl (1997, p. 8) provided some examples of this in his book, *Are We Scaring Ourselves to Death?*:

> For example, we fear radiation, which is known to cause cancer (as the media relentlessly tell us). Therefore, when it comes time to have a mammogram, a woman refuses because she fears the radiation exposure from the X ray. However, the risk of the radiation dose is miniscule compared to the benefits of finding a cancerous breast tumor before it becomes life-threatening. This woman quite literally could be scaring herself to death.
>
> A heterosexual man could be so nervous about contracting AIDS heterosexually—a tiny, tiny risk—that he never dates anyone and never marries. To avoid the minimal risk of contracting AIDS, he experiences the far greater risk of remaining single. Many studies have shown that single men experience more depression and poorer health than do married men.
>
> A teenage girl is frightened by the stories she reads in magazines about pesticides on fruits and vegetables, even though the pesticide risk is very small and deemed safe by the federal government. Soon she develops many nutritional imbalances and damages her internal organs. All this comes from not eating fruits and vegetables—the healthiest, most nutrition-packed foods available—thanks to her excessive fears of media-hyped pesticides.

As these examples show, unlike our ancestral predecessors, most of the demands we face today are ambiguous. It's a straightforward matter to appraise an onrushing tiger as a threat. But it's a little more difficult to make accurate appraisals when the source of the threat comes from the job market, the stock market, or the supermarket. It's worse still when we have to weigh carefully to choose between two or more potential threats. Should I take a new job, or hope that I will get promoted in my current job? Should I buy fruits and vegetables that may have been sprayed with pesticides, or purchase the more expensive organic variety? Am I making the right financial investments for the future? At least tiger-related threats are over quickly, and there is little doubt about whether they are handled successfully. But evaluating the differing methods for attaining financial security? You could spend years reading about this topic and still feel confused!

A major difficulty in accurately appraising demands is to know where to focus your energies. The quote that introduced this chapter, from late Supreme Court Justice Holmes, was "most people think dramatically, not quantitatively." What Holmes meant is that most people have a hard time being objective about the everyday risks in their lives. We are often fearful of things that are extremely unlikely to occur while we neglect very real threats to our well-being that often could be prevented if we weren't so busy overlooking them. Perhaps some of this is due to our biological heritage: When living in the jungle with hungry tigers, it is probably best to think "dramatically," since there was no shortage of dramatic events that could do you in.

Another reason we probably think dramatically is the pervasive influence of the modern media, including the entertainment industry. Nightly news shows are replete with victims of shootings and automobile fatalities, but offer a dearth of information on other common, but less dramatic, risks such as heart disease, depression, or social isolation. Larry Laudan, a professor of philosophy, attempted to shed some light on the real risks the average American faces in his work, *The Book of Risks* (1994). The following lists present some of the risks that an average American runs in any given year, as well as those risks the average American runs over a lifetime:

Yearly risks

- Someone will attack you with a deadly weapon: 1 in 261.

- You will die of heart disease: 1 in 340.

- You will die of cancer: 1 in 500.

- You will die from a stroke: 1 in 7,000.

- You will be murdered: 1 in 11,000.

- You will die in an airplane crash: 1 in 250,000.

- You will die in your bathtub: 1 in 1,000,000.

- You will be killed by lightning: 1 in 2,000,000.

- You will be killed by a tornado: 1 in 2,000,000.

Risks Over a Lifetime

- You will die of heart disease: 1 in 3.

- You will be the victim of a violent crime: 1 in 3.

- You will die of cancer: 1 in 5.

- You will be raped (if you're female): 1 in 11.

- You will die from a stroke: 1 in 14.

- You will go to prison (if you're male): 1 in 40.

- You will die in an auto accident: 1 in 45.

- You will be murdered: 1 in 93.

- You will die of AIDS: 1 in 97.

- You will die in an airplane crash: 1 in 4,000.

These statistics show that some of the events popularized in recent years in movies and television, such as killer tornadoes, are extremely unlikely to occur, whereas other risks, such as being involved in an auto accident, are far more likely. Most movies and television programs give you the idea that acts of violence are incredibly common, while less exciting and novel events, such as physical illness, are strikingly absent.

As an example, Chris was about ten years old when the movie *Jaws* came out. It became one of the first big summer blockbusters. Although his parents wouldn't let him see the movie at the time, he soaked up enough of the story line from friends and television commercials to know that he had no business going anywhere near the ocean, even though his family spent virtually every weekend at the Delaware shore. For an entire summer, he avoided going anywhere near the ocean because of the grossly exaggerated risk of getting attacked by a shark promulgated by the movie. He more or less ruined a summer at the beach avoiding a "risk" that probably happened to only a handful of people in the entire *world* that year.

The point is that we must consider carefully what we choose to spend our energy worrying about—all too often we are unnecessarily encouraged to react stressfully to unlikely problems.

Phantom Demands Can Be Costly

Our tremendous powers of reasoning, planning, and foresight can sometimes get us into trouble. Inordinate worrying can be costly in terms of time, energy, and money.

The widespread fear that computers would cease to function at the stroke of midnight on January 1, 2000, is a good example. The United States spent an estimated $100 billion on so-called "Y2K" preparedness while many other nations spent only a tiny fraction of this. When the hour of reckoning finally rolled around, it seemed that all nations fared equally well in avoiding computer complications associated with Y2K. The countries that spent little time or money worrying about Y2K did just as well as Americans, who seemed to obsess about it. The enormous amounts of time and money that many Americans spent getting U.S. computers ready for this phantom crisis, not to mention the time and money spent preparing for feared interruptions in the delivery of power, water, and food, was, in a sense, wasted.

While you can't stick your head in the sand to avoid problems, it is important to realize that when you spend your energy gearing up for one potential problem, you are using time and energy that becomes unavailable for other activities. Many times this occurs without your conscious awareness—you can become so used to being under heavy demands that you aren't even aware of the toll it takes on your health. Stress monitoring is an extremely useful method for detecting when demand levels are beginning to affect your well-being.

Monitoring Stress Arousal

The pace of life for many people is so swift that they remain unaware of the early stages of stress buildup. They dutifully jump from one task to the next without monitoring their own stressful sensations. Awareness is the first step in preventing serious bouts with stress. Awareness early in the stress cycle offers lead time for drawing on your coping resources and for avoiding or adjusting demand loads to maintain an optimal level of stimulation.

Optimal Stimulation for Minimal Stress

You must monitor your demand load to achieve optimal stimulation. *Optimal stimulation* doesn't mean maximal stimulation. Optimal stimulation refers to the amount of stimulation with which we function best—neither too much nor too little. This idea was first expressed in the Yerkes-Dodson Performance Curve in 1905. It demonstrates that performance generally improves as stimulation increases up to a point and then falls off with additional levels of stimulation or pressure. Similarly, increasing demands are associated with increases in one's coping efforts up to a point. You probably know intuitively that there is a limit to your ability to perform well under increasing amounts of stimulation. You also may sense that your performance suffers if the stimulation drops (and remains) below a certain level. Most people agree that boredom also is stressful. Thus, it is possible to be stressed by either too much or too little stimulation—by over-challenge *or* under-challenge. When you operate within your optimum range, you tend to flow with your work, your mood states are upbeat, and you experience a general sense of well-being. Figure 4-2 depicts this relationship.

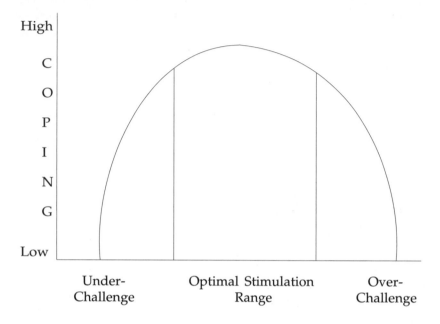

Figure 4-2. Optimal stimulation range.

Achieving optimal stimulation involves monitoring present levels of pressure, modifying demand levels, and adjusting the pace of your efforts. The test for determining your optimal stimulation range is personal and subjective. Perhaps you have a general idea of that point in demand buildup where you begin to show stress symptoms such as attention deficits, intolerance for interruptions, or a general sense of malaise. At the other end of the demand continuum you may be aware of times when too little is going on to interest you, when you need more rather than fewer demands to perk you up. Obviously these measurements are inexact, but some careful attention to body sensations when experiencing various levels of stimulation can help to sharpen your awareness of the optimal range.

Practice Body Scanning

You must learn to monitor early signs of stress arousal in order to make proper adjustments in your demand levels. This requires body scanning; that is, monitoring the sensations your body is experiencing. Your body will tell you when the level of stimulation is excessive or inadequate, but often, we are so driven by our pursuits and projects that we suppress the body's signals.

Careful attention to the early signs of arousal can make coping efforts earier and more successful. At the early stage of pressure buildup, efforts to relax are a great deal more effective. It is considerably more difficult to relax once the muscles are clamped in the vicelike grip of a stressful situation.

Form the habit of checking in on yourself from time to time during the day. We often ask others how they are but fail to check up on how we are feeling. Ask what your muscles are telling you. Identifying muscles that are beginning to grow tense and relaxing them will help to keep you loose all day. To monitor for stress arousal, scan the body for muscle tension. Focus your attention on your muscles, beginning with those in the head area. Move to the neck and shoulders, and then on to your upper and lower arms. Continue downward until your attention has encompassed all the muscle groups throughout your body. Sometimes it is easier to learn body scanning in the context of relaxation training. In part II, you will learn deep muscle relaxation. During this procedure, you are asked to first tense a muscle before relaxing it. The contrast between tension and relaxation becomes clearer this way. Practicing this form of muscle relaxation will greatly improve your awareness of developing stressful reactions.

Adjust Demand Levels

Roughly 75 percent of the life changes you checked on the Social Readjustment Rating Scale are self-selected! We tend to blame the elusive "they" for the pressure of events, but we ourselves are mostly responsible. Effective stress management requires spacing the demands you take on to insure that the load falls comfortably within your optimal stimulation range. For example, if you are experiencing heavy stressors at work, save the divorce until next year!

Check Your Pacing

You must also adjust your efforts to insure an even pace to avoid becoming harried. You have undoubtedly heard the old saying, "The hurrieder I get, the behinder I am." It is true that a maddening pace often creates additional stress. Do you hurry through your day? We often hurry because we are not invested in what we are doing; we just want to be through with it. This impatient hurrying makes for mistakes and accidents and creates a foul mood. We are more apt to approach our work in an unstressed manner if we are committed to it. This means we will have chosen the work because we believe it is important. Perhaps we would be better off if we made more conscious choices as to what is worth our time and efforts.

Rapid Shifts in Pacing May Be Dangerous

Donald Dudley, M.D., extended the work of his mentor, Thomas Holmes, creator of the SRRS. Along with his coauthor, Elton Welke, he examined the effects of rapid shifts between intense activity and withdrawal (1977). They found that stressful outcomes, such as illness, are not so much determined by the extent of the demand load as by the rapidity of shifts between activation and withdrawal. Sustained high or low activity levels were not as hurtful as rapid shifts between these levels. Perhaps this explains why retirement kills. Some life expectancy studies suggest that persons who continue to work in old age tend to live up to four years longer than persons who retire. Additionally, students often report more illnesses between semesters than during them. Dudley and Welke even suggested that illnesses associated with rapid withdrawal from heavy activity were more serious than those associated with rapid increases in activity.

Dudley and Welke are not suggesting that variation in activity levels is unhealthy, only rapid shifts in activity levels. Indeed, Selye suggested that variation in activity was a promising stress management technique, and the English historian Toynbee (1972) wrote that effective people always pursue a rhythm of activity and withdrawal. It's as though we go out to battle, and then we return to refurbish our equipment. The issue here, according to Dudley and Welke, is not high versus low levels of activity, but the rapidity of the activity-withdrawal cycling. Jerking the body in and out of high activation strains the body's ability to adjust to such changes, and systems maintaining its healthy condition begin to break down.

Avoiding Stressors

The better part of valor often is to avoid unnecessary battles. The lives of some people are cluttered up with unnecessary demands that create a sense of overload. This busy lifestyle may make them feel important and productive, but it unfortunately may distract them from troubling issues in their lives that need attention.

Avoid Stress by Wise Decision-Making

Because you face hundreds of decisions each year, you cannot possibly optimize your decisions by taking a deliberate, exhaustive approach to each of them. Some life decisions, however, are more important than others. Choose the wrong occupation, the wrong life partner, or make an unwise investment, and you may create an endless string of future stressors. Consequently, learning proper decision-making skills and taking the time and energy to use them when facing critical decisions can prevent much stress later. Three of the more important steps in wise decision-making are 1) clearly defining the problem; 2) identifying a fair representation of available options; and 3) committing yourself to a course of action.

Defining the problem.

The most common error in decision-making is the failure to properly define the problem. If you inaccurately define the problem, then *all* options will be inappropriate. We sometimes attempt to avoid the real problem by projecting the responsibility for it onto others. A husband may conclude that his wife's spendthrift behavior is to fault for their financial troubles, although he routinely loses heavily at the weekly poker game with his friends. A college student may believe that her roommate's social life is the reason for her failing marks, although she spends an inordinate amount of time on the web's chat rooms. Projecting the problem onto others may reduce your sense of guilt and offer you a free ticket for complaining, but it does little to solve the problem. The first step, therefore, is to honestly examine how *your* behavior contributes to the problem.

Avoid calling every difficulty in your life a problem to be solved. Some difficult situations cannot be *solved*; they are unpleasant situations out of your control, situations with which you must cope. Holding yourself responsible for solving it only adds to your self-criticism. If you are uncertain whether the situation can be remedied, turn it over in your mind and discuss it with trusted friends or professionals to hone in more accurately on the actual dimensions of the situation.

Identify options.

Perhaps the second most frequent cause of flawed decisions results from the failure to actively seek for alternative solutions. Failure to identify a full complement of options may come from a lazy, undisciplined approach to problem-solving, or it may be a response to the discomfort caused by indecision. Unresolved issues create tension, and to remove the tension you may quickly decide on a course of action. Unfortunately, most people when making decisions, even important ones, are prone to choose the first option that has a reasonable chance of being satisfactory. Nietzsche (1954) said, "The first representation that explains the unknown as familiar feels so good that one considers it true." Although the immediate result of this impulsivity is anxiety reducing, the long-range effect may multiply our stressors. It is best to suffer the tension from an unresolved issue long enough to identify a more promising set of options.

Commit yourself to a course of action.

Once you have identified a range of reasonable options, select one and commit yourself to making it work. Although your discomfort when facing problems may prompt you sometimes to make decisions prematurely, at other times a lack of confidence may cause you to inappropriately delay making the decision. Procrastination may result from either of two causes. First, you may put off making a decision for fear of having your choice evaluated by others. The thinking seems to be, "If I don't make the decision, then others cannot judge me." The fear of a negative reaction from others may freeze you into inactivity. Secondly, procrastination may signal an unwillingness to give up other alternatives. A choice *for* one alternative is a choice *against* all other alternatives. So, as long as you don't make a decision, you haven't lost your options.

Avoid Ego Struggles

Many stressful encounters with others are useless ego struggles where the only prize is the protection of your self-image. You argue about trivial issues that don't *really* matter. The point of the argument is actually to decide who is to be declared the victor, to be declared "right." As pointed out in *A Course in Miracles* (Schucman and Thetford 1976), you sometimes act as though it's more important to be *right* than *happy*. It almost seems as if you would rather an ominous prediction come true so you can be proven right, than for things to turn out happily for you. You want to feel a certain way about yourself, and you insist that others help you by supporting your inflexible views. It is best to avoid the tendency to convince others when it is not critical to your well-being. Doing so will help you escape a great deal of unnecessary stress. Seek out win-win solutions to mutual problems. *Compromise is* not a dirty word. To prevent stress from these damaging ego struggles, take yourself less seriously. An Atlanta disc jockey had it right when he said, "The thing that most determines how many people will attend your funeral is *the weather!"*

Sending "I" Messages

You can avoid a lot of stressful encounters with others by taking responsibility for your reactions. This approach is sometimes referred to as sending "I" messages rather than "you" messages. Instead of saying, "You get me upset when you don't close the garage door," you could say, "I get upset when you don't close the garage door." Instead of saying, "You irritate me with your loudness," you could say, "I become uncomfortable when you yell so loudly." These changes in expression may seem like subtle differences, but the impact on the other person is less irritating.

It is impossible to cope effectively with stress without an accurate reading on your demands. The first half of this book has helped you gain an understanding of your life demands and the ways they may be causing you stress. Remember, the invisible tigers that threaten you today are mostly the function of your perceptions. To tame them, you must first make sure your perceptions are accurate.

Even those with abundant coping resources will encounter many demands significant enough to represent a source of stress in life. This is the focus of part II. In chapter 5 we will extend the road map first presented in chapter 3 so that it encompasses methods for coping with stressful situations. To cope successfully, however, you must build your coping resources, such as those addressed in chapter 6. You'll find suggestions for building a rich array of resources, including wellness, interpersonal skills, relaxation procedures, and methods for deepening spirituality. Later chapters will examine stress-inducing personalities (chapter 7), methods for overcoming stressful patterns of thinking (chapter 8), and practices that create stress-free consciousness (chapter 9). Finally chapter 10 presents step-by-step instructions for using the many coping methods we'll discuss.

Part II

Coping with Stress

Chapter 5

Road Map for Coping

An undefined problem has an infinite number of solutions.

—Robert A. Humphrey

*I find that the great thing in this world is not so much where
we stand as in what direction we are moving; to reach the port
of heaven, we must sail sometimes with the wind and sometimes
against it—but we must sail, and not drift, nor lie at anchor.*

—Oliver Wendell Holmes

We encounter many life demands each day. We handle most of them
well, but if a demand threatens to outstrip our ability to cope with

it—boom! We've got ourselves a stressor. Once a stressor pops up on the radar screen, there are two ways to deal with it: either attempt to fight it or attempt to live with it. As we've already suggested, attempts to combat a stressor are called *problem-focused* coping, and attempts to live with a stressor are called *emotion-focused* coping.

Many stressors call for both problem- and emotion-focused coping behaviors. Confronting a roommate over late rent payments is one example. If you sit down and figure out exactly what part of the rent your roommate owes, what you want to say to your roommate, and the best time to say it, that's problem-focused coping. You are dealing directly with the problem.

However, your efforts to present your case in the most diplomatic manner may be undermined by your intense desire to "ring your roommate's neck." Every time you add up her tardy fees, your stomach may knot up, your jaws may clench, and your head may be filled with graphic images of just what you'd like to do to her. Some emotion-focused coping is clearly called for here. Maybe you go out and take a walk or even pound a couch pillow a few times before your roommate gets home, but there's no way your talk with your roommate is going to be productive unless you cool down a bit. In this way, emotion- and problem-focused coping behaviors actually complement each other, each making the other more effective. Cooling yourself down emotionally before a confrontation allows you to get your message across more effectively. And successfully communicating with others can alleviate the problem, removing stress-produced emotions.

This chapter offers suggestions for both problem- and emotion-focused coping, as well as suggestions for deciding in a

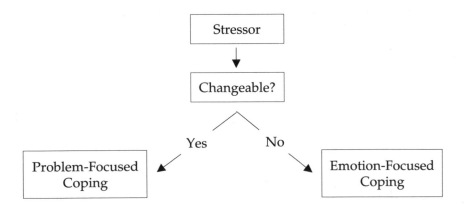

Figure 5-1. Decision tree for choice of coping strategy.

given case which mode of coping is most useful. The bottom line is whether or not you can really do anything about the problem. If you can resolve the problem situation, and the cost is not too great in doing so, by all means do it! Eliminating problems saves tremendous amounts of energy in the long run. However, if you cannot change the situation, at least in the shortrun, emotion-focused coping is called for. This relationship is presented in Figure 5-1 above.

The Bias in Favor of Problem-Focused Coping

Although we generally recommend the use of problem-focused coping, life sometimes presents you with situations and events that cannot be readily "solved." It is unrealistic to equate successful coping only with the *elimination* of life demands. Instead, you must be able to pick and choose when it is most appropriate to combat a stressor and when the prudent course is to "live with it." The best solution of all is prevention, which we will discuss in later chapters. But people often exaggerate their ability to control their environments and therefore make ineffective use of problem-focused efforts at coping. This exaggerated sense of control over your environment seems to operate at the cultural level as well. For example, one of the biggest complaints that veterans of military service have about Hollywood war films is that they consistently portray soldiers in combat as having more control over battlefield conditions than occurs in real life. Movies usually portray soldiers who know exactly where the enemy is, how to sneak up on them, and how to dispatch them. However, survivors of real wars know the truth: Contact with the enemy often involves utter confusion and unpredictability. Soldiers often get lost, equipment breaks down, and when actual shooting starts, chaos often rules. This is understandable, for audiences usually expect to be entertained by films that celebrate the heroics of soldiers, not ones that portray the horror and unpredictable nature of war.

In a similar way, many people have false impressions about how to successfully cope with stress. Many people fervently look for easy ways to exert complete control over their environments. Unfortunately, it's often not that easy. Successful coping often requires the ability to live peacefully with problems that can't be easily solved. With this caveat in mind, let us look more carefully at your two options for coping with stressors: problem-focused and emotion-focused coping.

Problem-Focused Coping

Although there are problems associated with using either problem-focused or emotion-focused coping exclusively, under most circumstances it is preferable to favor problem-focused approaches. Passive approaches to coping have a greater likelihood of inducing depression and lessening the effectiveness of the immune system in fighting cancer and infectious diseases (Antoni 1987). Moreover, relying on emotion-focused coping when problem-focused coping is reasonable means that you will deal with the stressor for a much longer period. The net result will be a greater expenditure of coping resources.

Heavy Demands Plus Control Increases Resistance to Illness

We cannot be certain that busy people are stressed people and that busyness will lead to illness. High demand levels *with perceived control* actually may fortify your immune system. Steven Locke (1986) studied the effects of stressful life events on the immune functioning of Harvard undergraduates. Students in his study had high scores on an adaptation of the Social Readjustment Rating Scale. This indicated that they had experienced a large number of life changes over the previous year. He surveyed these students for signs of anxiety and/or depression. Students reporting high levels of anxiety or depression were considered poor copers and those reporting little or no anxiety or depression as good copers. He assessed the efficiency of the immune systems of these students by measuring the number and activity of natural killer (NK) cells that fight cancer and viruses. There were distinct differences between the poor and good copers. The poor copers had lower NK cell counts, and when a NK cell was drawn from the blood and placed in the presence of an infectious agent, it was sluggish in its attack. The good copers, however, showed *higher* immune cell activity, even higher than for students who experienced *few* life demands and reported *low* levels of anxiety and depression!

It seems likely that the poor copers in this study, who were experiencing anxiety and/or depression in the face of high demands, had perceived these demands to be beyond their control and had adopted passive modes for coping with them. Michael Antoni (1987) found that passive coping is more likely to interfere with immune functioning than active coping. Indeed, he found that both the neurology and chemistry of the stress response are quite different for passive and active copers. Active coping requires a greater role for the sympathetic nervous system and the catecholamines, norepinephrine and epinephrine, whereas passive coping requires a greater role for the pituitary gland and corticosteroids, such as cortisol. Corticosteroids have been associated with lower immune defense and increased vulnerability to infectious diseases and cancer. An elevated level of cortisol often is an earmark of mental depression, and depression also is associated with higher rates of cancer.

In contrast to Locke's poor copers, the good copers likely perceived their demands to be within their control and coped actively with them. If so, they would have experienced higher levels of sympathetic nervous system activity, but lower levels of corticosteroid production—a combination of physiological changes that does *not* appear to lower immune functioning. The Harvard study seems to suggest that high demand levels may serve as a kind of watershed—with poor copers viewing them as stressors and experiencing lowered immune functioning, and with good copers viewing the demands as challenges and gearing up in a healthy way to deal with them. Both Antoni's analysis and Locke's research are compatible with the research of Matheny and Cupp discussed earlier in this chapter. Albert Bandura (1982), a researcher famous for his work on self-efficacy, came to the same conclusion when he suggested that personal efficacy (a sense of control or mastery) is the single most effective buffer against the hurtful effects of stress.

A *sense* of control is helpful in lowering stress, even when the control is not supported by the facts. In one study (Glass and Singer 1972), clerical workers were exposed to loud noises while they performed certain clerical tasks. Later when given a proofreading assignment, they made more errors than coworkers who also were exposed to the noises but were told that they could turn off the noise by pressing a button (even though the button did not actually control the noise). As another example, although it is estimated that the chances of experiencing injury or death is ten times greater while traveling a standard distance by auto than by airplane, many persons are much more fearful of flying than driving. Many people are less afraid in heavy traffic if they have their hands on the wheel than if they are in the passenger's seat. Although a sense of control usually lowers or prevents stress, there is one circumstance in which it may actually increase the intensity of the stress response—believing you have control over an uncontrollable situation. The immediate effect of the belief may be stress reducing, but the belief may trigger higher intensities of the stress response as it becomes clear that the stressor is uncontrollable (Sapolsky 1998, p. 226).

It is important to note that emotion-focused coping does not necessarily mean passive coping. The key dimension is a sense of control. The control may be directed either to attacks on the problem or to the control of your emotional response—or to control of both. Mastery over either stressful demands or your emotional reactions to them promotes a healthy sense of control. Many times it is more difficult to control your own damaging emotional reactions than to control the external situation. Much attention has been devoted to thought and emotional control in religious and consciousness disciplines. We will discuss emotion-focused control later in this chapter and return to this subject, along with the subject of thought control, in chapters 8 and 9.

Problem-focused coping may take many forms. Some forms are specific, such as joining a weight-control program, following a prescribed medical regimen, fixing a broken part, or allowing more time to travel from one place to another. Others, however, are more general. Three general strategies for attacking stressors are problem-solving, resolving interpersonal conflicts, and making more efficient use of your time.

Problem-Solving

In some cases successful coping may require problem-solving and decision-making. The textbook steps involved include: clearly defining the problem, seeking information and advice regarding the problem, identifying alternative courses of action for eliminating the problem, estimating the merit of such alternatives, taking action based on the most promising alternative, monitoring the results, and revising the course of action as necessary. Most people do not approach problems in such a rigorous, conscious manner. They generally take a more intuitive approach to problem-solving. For most problems, this intuitive approach works okay, but with problems that have long-range implications for your welfare, the results could be highly distressing. The most common deficits in problem-solving involve three of the above steps—namely, failure to clearly identify the problem, failure to identify a sufficient number of alternative courses of action, and failure to adjust the course of action based on feedback.

Resolving Interpersonal Conflicts

Much stress comes from interpersonal conflicts. Most of our needs are met in a social context, and our needs sometimes conflict with the needs of others. The resulting conflicts create stress. If you have made an unfortunate choice of companions, or if you have failed to develop social skills such as negotiation skills, listening skills, or assertiveness skills, you may experience a great deal of inter-personal conflict. Incompatible relationships ensure ongoing frustra-tion and stress of varying degrees. Having the skills and the will to resolve conflicts is vitally important to successful stress management.

Time Management

The escalating demands of modern living ravenously consume our time. The pace of life speeds up as we attempt to live the lives of three people within the years allotted to one person. We can reduce the resulting stress by challenging the addictive need to constantly *do* and *acquire* more and more. It also helps to learn to use time more efficiently. The shelves of bookstores are stacked with volumes on time management, and there are endless seminars on the subject. The inefficient use of time often results from a failure to clearly set goals and to prioritize the tasks for reaching them.

Emotion-Focused Coping

The other major type of coping, emotion-focused coping, is most use-ful for demands that you cannot change. Ordinary difficulties that must be lived with may turn into bigger problems if you don't accept their irresolvability (Watzlawick, Weakland, and Fisch 1974). You may create considerable stress for yourself in trying to solve such problems. Grief caused by the loss of a loved one cannot be solved. Growing old cannot be solved. Terminal cancer and the suffering that accompanies it cannot be solved. None of these conditions has solutions. They are inescapable human predicaments with which we must learn to live. Treating them as though they are problems that can be solved is a serious mistake.

Remember the St. Francis of Assisi prayer that was introduced back in chapter 3? We need wisdom to know the difference between the things we can change and the things we cannot. For example, when it became known that basketball superstar Magic Johnson had tested postive for HIV antibodies, his former teammate from the Los Angeles Lakers, Kareem Abdul-Jabbar, announced that the news caused him to think about ending his retirement and making a pro-fessional comeback. It is hard to see how this attempt to restart his basketball career could have helped his sick friend, but it is clear that Abdul-Jabbar wanted to do *something*. Although he never did attempt a comeback, Kareem's intentions may be seen as a noble attempt at problem-focused coping when in fact no such option existed.

Many of the most famous and powerful seem to have similar difficulties in handling situations that do not lend themselves to problem-focused solutions. However, at times, your personal values may also restrain you from taking more active approaches to solving your problems. Consider the example of a young woman who complained to her therapist that she was living with her husband in a state of quiet desperation. She saw herself as vibrant, outgoing, and somewhat experimental, while she pictured her husband as a good, responsible man, but with minimal needs for intimacy. She felt herself drying up psychologically for lack of touch, warmth, and sharing. She had disclosed her unmet needs to him, but each time he had become embarrassed and changed the subject.

Although divorce had crossed her mind many times, her personal values effectively kept her from taking such action. She was a deeply committed Roman Catholic and respected the Church's proscription against divorce. She saw herself as a kind, considerate wife who could never hurt a husband who didn't deserve such treatment, and as a loving, responsible mother who would not cause suffering for her children to meet her selfish needs. Her values were as effective as steel bands in restraining her from seeking a divorce.

When faced with such irresolvable stressors, you must turn to emotion-focused coping. Some of the strategies used in attempting to control your emotions include striving to accept the inevitable, reframing the situation in ways that will reduce the suffering, suppressing stressful thoughts that merely fuel stress, discharging painful emotions, learning to distinguish sensations from emotions, practicing relaxation techniques, and using exercise to lower uncomfortable physical arousal.

Accepting the Inevitable

It is generally easier for "externals" to accept uncontrollable stressors than for "internals." "Internals" are people who believe they are mainly responsible for what happens to them. "Externals," on the other hand, assign a much larger role to luck, fate, or chance in accounting for what happens to them. Much of the time the belief in your ability to master the environment leads to greater effort and greater success. When the situation is inevitable and uncontrollable, it is wiser to accept the situation than to fight it.

Don't Discount the Importance of Hope

Hope is a powerful ally in dealing with stressors. The perception that events are improving significantly reduces stress. We are better able to tolerate stressful conditions if we believe things will get better. The ability to look forward to tomorrow may increase or reduce stress depending upon our reading. If we conclude that things are never going to get better, the present distress intensifies. Believing that "This too shall pass" and that in time things will improve lessens the stressfulness of the situation.

Reframing

Reframing is a matter of looking at a situation or event differently so as to change its meaning. It is a most promising coping strategy since the stress response is triggered by our appraisals. Your emotional responses to situations and events largely are determined by the meaning you assign to them. Consequently, if you change the meaning, you change the emotion. The new frames within which the situation is viewed might conform more *or less* to reality. It is possible to deny reality in an effort to make yourself feel better. The use of such unrealistic frames might calm the emotions temporarily, but their unrealistic basis is likely to be uncovered by developing events. Because we often exaggerate the negative aspects of events, however, a reframe has the likelihood of being *more* realistic than the frame we originally chose. The positive effects of reframing are evident in the case of a young law student who was concerned about a problem with "sexual inadequacy."

Actually it was a problem with premature ejaculation. Premature ejaculation occurs as a result of the person fearing that the ejaculation will come before his partner experiences an orgasm. The law student was a handsome, bright, outgoing young man who had no difficulty getting dates. However, he experienced deep shame when his sexual engagements ended abruptly with his untimely ejaculations. He was greatly troubled by his "failures" and felt he was permanently flawed.

When asked to describe a typical sexual engagement, he offered the following account. The evening ordinarily went smoothly through dinner and the subsequent approach behaviors. His partner would usually be receptive to his sexual advances. Soon, however, he would begin to fear his usual fate and would desperately try to delay ejaculation. Typically he was unsuccessful. He would ejaculate before his partner could experience orgasm, and he became ashamed and depressed. He then would sit on the bedside with hands covering his face and apologize profusely to his partner. Often his partner would attempt to reassure him, but this embarrassing attention only deepened his shame.

The young law student was encouraged to reframe his "problem differently." It was suggested that his "sexual inadequacy" was a misnomer, and that a better description of his behavior was "sexual hypersensitivity." He was told that many men now taking Viagra would dearly love to have his problem, that his body was working just fine, and that he was delightfully responsive to the sensuality of his partners. The underlying physiology of the orgasm was explained, including how fearful thoughts could themselves trigger an ejaculation prematurely. The reframe, then, pictured him as a healthy, vibrant young man who was highly responsive to female sensuality. Nature had beautifully equipped him for sexual pleasure. He was in no way "sexually inadequate." His only problem was his runaway thoughts about untimely ejaculations.

The client accepted the reframe but asked how this new understanding would bring his ejaculations under control. It was suggested that he also should reframe his view of what his sexual partners were wanting. His partners, of course, wanted to experience an orgasm, but they were not concerned that the orgasms be simultaneous—that, in fact, the orgasms of sexual partners often are not simultaneous. It was explained to him that he created his social awkwardness by his behavior *after his ejaculation.* Because he believed that it was necessary to synchronize his ejaculation with the female's orgasm, he experienced, *and clearly displayed*, shame at his "failure." His embarrassment quite likely destroyed the sexual interest of his partner.

An alternative set of behaviors was suggested to him. If he prematurely ejaculated, he was to say something to his partner like, "My God, you're so beautiful and sensual! When I feel your warm body, I can't control myself." Then, he was to continue pleasuring his companion until she experienced an orgasm as well. He was greatly relieved by the explanation and enthusiastically sought an opportunity to try out this new pattern of behavior. He didn't get the opportunity to put in place the entire plan, however, because he did *not* ejaculate prematurely during his next sexual encounter! The reframe of his behavior coupled with his plan for handling the situation if he ejaculated prematurely removed his fear and allowed him to enjoy the experience more fully.

Suppressing Distressing Thoughts

People often consciously suppress thoughts about distressing situations or events in order to control their emotional responses. Many times this emotion-focused coping strategy is wise. If you have have done all you can to resolve the stressful situation, then further processing of the situation may merely make matters worse. Because the body doesn't know the difference between fact and fantasy, it treats as reality whatever pictures the mind creates. The continuous reprocessing of stressful situations creates an ever-deepening slough of despondency.

Suppressing distressing thoughts, however, may interfere with taking action to deal realistically with the situation. This clearly was the case with a woman who for years denied the significance of a thyroid goiter. As unbelievable as it may seem, the goiter grew exceedingly large and unsightly, but she still continued to avoid medical attention. Eventually, she was forcibly taken to the hospital from weakness, excessive weight loss, and pain. The diagnosis: Cancer of the thyroid and colon, and a subsequent examination revealed a carcinoma on her back as well. She later confessed that the lesion on her back had been developing for years, and that she had hidden the skin lesion from her husband all the while. For years the woman had refused to deal with the seriousness of her condition, and her denial resulted in her death. Appropriate problem-focused coping, in this case actively seeking medical attention, well might have spared her life.

Discharging Painful Emotions

A person may become unhappy or ill from bottled-up emotions. Disclosing your feelings to interested parties, whether friends, family, or professional helpers, often provides great relief. Maintaining a "stiff upper lip," suffering in silence, may be endorsed in certain cultures, but it doesn't seem wise from what we know about human emotions. Emotions create biochemicals, and persistent negative emotions conduct a kind of chemical warfare against the body. Many people are reluctant to bother others with their problems, and some fail to use their social support networks because they don't want others to know they have problems. They seem to be favoring their egos over the welfare of their bodies.

Self-disclosure

Dr. James Pennebaker is a social psychologist who has devoted the last fifteen years to exploring the nature of self-disclosure and physical health. In a fascinating series of studies, Pennebaker and his colleagues have shown that expressing emotions appears to protect the body from stress and results in significant long-term health benefits. One of the primary mechanisms used to accomplish this end is the practice of journaling. In numerous studies, Pennebaker found that participants who were asked to write about upsetting experiences, ranging from relationship difficulties to more extreme forms of trauma, actually experienced greater health as measured by visits to the doctor and other indices of well-being. Pennebaker (1997) offers the following suggestions for using journaling as a way to cope with negative experiences and emotions.

- Write about topics or events that you are currently dealing with, not necessarily those that are the most upsetting or traumatic. Simply writing about your deepest emotions and thoughts regarding an event or circumstance that is causing difficulty or draining your energy will lessen the intensity of your reaction.

- When and where: It usually is not necessary to write for long periods. Usually fifteen minutes or so is sufficient, and don't worry about spelling or grammar. Pennebaker has found significant health benefits for individuals who wrote for only a few fifteen minute sessions. Writing may benefit you most when it's done in a unique or novel setting where you won't be interrupted or distracted.

- You do not need to share what you have written with others. The benefits of therapeutic writing are not dependent on others reading what you have written. Planning to show your writing to others may also interfere with your level of self-disclosure.

- Writing about upsetting experiences may actually dampen your mood for a few hours or even a day. However, in the long run it leads to feelings of relief and contentment. Your long-term health can also be enhanced.

Distinguishing Sensations from Emotions

Pain treatment centers often train patients with intractable pain to recognize the sensations without referring to them in such a way as to add emotional duress. Experts in these pain centers know that the experience of pain often has both physical and emotional contributors. For example, it is estimated that for the first few weeks after a spinal cord injury, roughly eighty percent of the pain is derived from nervous tissue damage and twenty percent from emotional reactions. After a few months, however, the relative contributions of physical and emotional factors to the pain is reversed— emotional factors account for roughly eighty percent and physical factors account for twenty percent. The same set of sensations may be described quite differently from person to person, and the label placed on the sensations seems to have a great deal to do with the amount of pain experienced.

Patients with unremitting lower back pain sometimes are taught to focus on the sensations rather than ignore them. They are asked to take on the role of dispassionate scientists in observing the throbbing sensations and the tightness of the muscles, but to do so *without thinking of these sensations as intolerable pain*. The goal here is to remove the contibution of emotional factors to the pain. It may seem to you that the approach is merely a game, worthless as an intervention. However, much evidence suggests that such approaches sometimes significantly moderate the discomfort.

This approach to the control of physical pain may prove helpful in dealing with psychological pain as well. Mark, an agoraphobic therapy client, was treated in this way. Agoraphobia is a fear of open spaces, and Mark feared driving on the expressways. He lived forty-five miles from his corporate office, and he needed to travel on an interstate highway to get there. The thought of being on the six-lane road terrified him, and on a number of occasions he panicked while driving. He would struggle to bring the automobile to a halt on the right shoulder, lock the car doors, walk to the nearest telephone and call his wife. She would ask a neighbor to accompany her to the site of the abandoned car and to drive it back home while she took her husband on to work. He was made to feel stupid and childish by his phobic response.

Once it was decided that there was no underlying motive for his difficulty in reaching his office, the problem was treated as a phobic response. Although a desensitization technique was originally used, the breakthrough came when Mark was asked to focus on the sensations he was experiencing while on the expressway. Whereas he typically tried to distract his attention from his growing arousal sensations, he now was asked to focus on these sensations *without concluding that he was panicking*. He was to focus keen attention on the tightness in his grip of the wheel, the deepening of his breathing, the tautness of muscles, and other sensations. He found that the sensations were tolerable as long as he didn't jump to the conclusion that he was panicking. Once he had drawn this distinction, his panicky reaction to driving on the expressway slowly disappeared.

Engaging in Relaxing Activities

One of the more common emotion-focused forms of coping is engaging in forms of relaxation. Some people relax by viewing television, listening to music, or reading a novel. Unfortunately, some persons rely exclusively on drugs to control their emotional responses. Alcohol has been a favorite choice for relaxing over the millennia. Although alcohol may be useful in lowering arousal if used in moderation (and at appropriate times), the drug has often been abused with disastrous results. A healthier approach is to pursue a formal relaxation procedure such as regulated breathing, deep muscle relaxation, autogenic training, yoga, or meditation. These practices are very effective in lowering inappropriate arousal and may retrain your nervous system to respond more appropriately after a reasonable period. We will discuss these relaxation procedures further in chapter 6.

Exercise

Because the stress response was bred into us to prepare us to respond physically to acute danger, vigorous exercise seems to be the natural way of lowering arousal. Aerobic exercise in particular has numerous relaxing properties and multiple positive effects on your health and functioning. Considerable attention is devoted to forms of exercise in chapter 6 as well.

Following the Road Map for Coping

We end this chapter by presenting a checklist for coping. Because stressors are so varied, it is impossible to outline a series of steps for coping that would be entirely appropriate for all situations. However, the behaviors on this checklist are often useful. The checklist assumes that you have appraised your demands as exceeding your resources, and consequently, you are no longer dealing with demands but rather with stressors. The checklist considers both those situations in which stressors are controllable (where problem-focused coping would be appropriate) and those that are not (where emotion-focused coping would be appropriate). The checklist will be more instructive if you have a specific stressful situation in mind—perhaps an interpersonal conflict, a health problem, or a serious financial bind. Check to see which of the steps would be appropriate in dealing with the stressor you have in mind. And now the checklist:

1. **Decide whether to combat the stressor or to declare détente.** Get an accurate reading on the stressor to decide whether you should attack it or merely live with it.

- This decision will rest on your judgment as to whether or not it is possible to change (control) the stressor. Ask, "Is there anything that I can constructively do?"

  - If "No," shift to emotion-focused coping.

  - If "Yes," then ask further, "Am I *willing* to take this action?"

    - If "Yes," then focus on problem-focused coping.

    - If "No," then shift to emotion-focused coping.

- Focus on the temporary nature of the stressor. There will be a natural tendency for you to think of the situation as permanent. Although a few stressors will be permanent, the vast majority of them are temporary. Remind yourself that "this too shall pass."

- Resist the tendency to globalize the stressor, to imagine that its effects spread across every part of your life. Place the stressor in proper perspective by acknowledging its temporality and its specificity.

2. **If you decide on problem-focused coping,** then consider the following:

- Accept emotionally beforehand the costs of this course of action. Much of your impatience in dealing with stressful conditions results from an unwillingness to accept what it will cost you to cope with it.

- Begin your response under favorable circumstances. Plan your attack on the stressor carefully, and choose to begin when your motivation is high.

- Prevent emotional hijacking by resisting the tendency to exaggerate the threat that the stressor poses and to discount your resources for handling it.

- Lower your emotional arousal. This will help to clarify your thinking. You may exercise or use a form of relaxation such as meditation, yoga, prayer, regulated breathing, deep muscle relaxation, autogenic training, or the quieting response to be helpful for this purpose. These practices will be explained in chapter 6.

- Inventory your coping resources. Ask yourself:

  - "What would I need to cope adequately with the situation?"

- "What resources do I have for coping with the situation?" (If you believe that your resources are insufficient, ask yourself how you can obtain the missing resources.)

- Have I dealt with similar stressors before?

- Who do I know that has dealt well with this situation?

- Next, take action! You have looked carefully at the stressor and your available resources; now commit yourself to a course of action that seems reasonable.

- Strengthen your resolve for action by motivational reading, celebrating your progress, and enlisting a network of caring others to encourage your efforts.

- Be willing to make necessary changes in your attack that were not anticipated in your original planning. This may mean altering your goals to develop alternative rewards, building social relationships, or engaging in substitute pursuits such as doing volunteer work or studying philosophy or religion.

3. **If you decide upon emotion-focused coping,** then consider the following:

- Resign yourself to the situation. You have decided that there is nothing reasonable that you can (and will) do about the situation. Consequently, you should make peace with yourself regarding the issue.

- Remind yourself that your goal is merely to take care of yourself, to try to regulate your emotions to reduce the emotional pain the stressor may cause you.

- Discharge painful emotions. Self-disclose your concerns to a close friend, spouse, family member, or professional helper. Airing your feelings often makes the stressful situation more tolerable.

- Pursue activities or practices that will center you, such as:

  - meditation

  - yoga

  - prayer

  - regulating breathing

  - deep muscle relaxation

- autogenic training

- the quieting response

- Reframe what you can't change. This may require you to become creative. Look for the good in the situation. Remind yourself that often, "The other side of a liability is an asset," and, "Crisis signals both danger and opportunity." One promising tact is to ask yourself, "What can I learn from this situation?"

- Engage in vigorous activity. This is nature's way of ridding the body of stress hormones. All physical activity is useful for this purpose, but aerobic exercise has a number of superior qualities when compared with other forms of exercise. We will discuss various forms of exercise in chapter 6 as well.

- Suppress stressful thoughts. Now that you've decided that nothing can be done about the situation and have disclosed your problem to caring others, protect your mood by suppressing thoughts of the problem. Repression (*unconscious* suppression of thoughts) is generally undesirable, but conscious suppression might be a useful way of redirecting your energy to more self-enhancing activities.

Your ability to cope with stressful events will depend to a large degree upon the adequacy of the resources that you possess. Highly resourceful people handle with ease and composure many events that seriously strain the resources of others. They view stressful situations as laboratories for further developing their coping resources. Mihaly Csikszentmihalyi (1990) refers to superior forms of coping as transformational. Superior copers transform the threatening situations into opportunities for self-development. People who approach life's difficulties in this way are survivors—they feed on their stressors! In the next chapter you will have the opportunity to inventory your coping resources, and we will offer suggestions for further enriching them.

Chapter 6

Building Stress-Coping Resources

The greatest pleasure in life is doing what people say you cannot do.

—Walter Bagehot

If the only tool you have is a hammer, you tend to see every problem as a nail.

—Abraham Maslow

The role of prevention in coping is often unrecognized and under-appreciated. People don't receive the Congressional Medal of Honor for preventing a crisis; they receive it for saving people from a disaster that has already happened. The real payoff of prevention, of course, is that it saves you from having to combat a stressor at all. Building additional coping resources and avoiding unnecessary stressors are the two most important forms of preventive coping. We discussed the importance of avoiding unnecessary stressors in chapter 4. In this chapter we discuss the importance of building a rich set of coping resources.

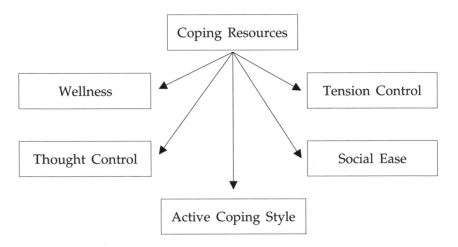

Figure 6-1. Coping resources.

Coping resources are factors in place *before* stressors occur. The effectiveness of your coping efforts will depend largely upon the richness of your coping resources. Antonovsky (1979) referred to these resources as *general resistance factors,* because they greatly enhance your resistance to the ill effects of stress. In the same way that a strong immune system protects you from illness, a rich set of coping resources prevents a great deal of stress. Figure 6-1 depicts the coping resources that we will discuss in this chapter.

Remember, the stress response is triggered when you conclude that your resources are inadequate for the demands you are facing. Steven Hobfoll (1989) argued that the assessment of your coping resources is a better predictor of stress symptoms than the assessment of demands. If you possess ample resources, fewer situations will appear stressful to you. Below is an inventory that will help you assess your coping resources. Answer each question carefully. Afterward score your responses by computing a separate score for each resource.

Stress Coping Resources Inventory:
A Self-Assessment

Instructions: People differ remarkably in their responses to potentially stressful events. For instance, about one in ten hostages comes out of captivity a mentally healthier person that when entering, while the others may face extreme emotional difficulty. What are the factors associated with coping success? The questions below relate to factors most closely associated with the capacity to cope successfully with stress. Circle the letter which lists the option that you choose. Answer each question as honestly as possible.

1. How frequently do you moderately exercise?

    a. daily or more often

    b. once or twice a week

    c. once or twice a month

    d. seldom

2. How often do you get a full, restful night of sleep?

    a. most every night

    b. four to five times each week

    c. two to three times each week

    d. seldom

3. To what extent is your energy sufficient for your work and daily activities?

    a. to a very great extent

    b. to some extent

    c. to little extent

    d. to very little extent

4. How closely does your weight approach the ideal level?

    a. My weight is at the ideal level.

    b. My weight is close to the ideal level.

    c. My weight is not close to the ideal level.

    d. I am dangerously overweight (or underweight).

5. To what extent do you eat a nutritious diet?

    a. to a very great extent

    b. to some extent

    c. to little extent

    d. to very little extent

6. Which of the following best describes your use of tobacco?

    a. In no period of my life have I had the habit of smoking or chewing tobacco.

    b. Early in my life for a short period I smoked or chewed tobacco.

    c. I stopped smoking or chewing tobacco over the past two years.

    d. I currently smoke or chew tobacco.

7. Which of the following best describes your use of alcohol?

    a. I do not abuse alcohol, and never have. (Abuse is defined as drinking more than two drinks within a short period such as an evening.)

    b. Very occasionally I abuse alcohol.

    c. I have a history of abusing alcohol, but am not presently abusing it.

    d. I am presently abusing alcohol.

8. To what extent do you believe that you have a history of coping well with highly stressful situations?

    a. to a very great extent

    b. to a great extent

    c. to little extent

    d. to very little extent

9. How confident are you of being able to control your emotions in stressful situations?

    a. I never let my emotions run away with me.

    b. I seldom let my emotions run away with me.

    c. I sometimes let my emotions run away with me.

    d. I often let my emotions run away with me.

10. When things are not going well, how likely are you to view the situation as being temporary rather than permanent?

    a. very likely

    b. likely

c. unlikely

d. very unlikely

11. When something bad happens to you, how likely are you to exaggerate its importance?

    a. very unlikely

    b. unlikely

    c. likely

    d. very likely

12. When stressed by a complex situation, how likely are you to focus your attention on those aspects of the situation that you can manage?

    a. very likely

    b. likely

    c. unlikely

    d. very unlikely

13. When highly stressed, how capable are you of changing your thinking to calm down?

    a. very capable

    b. capable

    c. incapable

    d. very incapable

14. When confronted with a stressful situation, how likely are you to wait passively for events to develop rather than to take charge?

    a. very unlikely

    b. unlikely

    c. likely

    d. very likely

15. Which of the following courses of action are you most likely to take when you have become thoroughly frustrated?

    a. identify an alternative goal and pursue it

    b. pursue a relaxing activity

    c. withdraw and feel sorry for yourself

    d. vent your aggression on someone weaker than yourself

16. If you had worn an article of clothing one day and then found it to be flawed, how likely would you be to return it and ask for a refund?

    a. very likely

    b. likely

    c. unlikely

    d. very unlikely

17. When an unexpected, negative event happens to you, how likely are you to actively seek information about the event and how to cope with it?

    a. very likely

    b. likely

    c. unlikely

    d. very unlikely

18. How much decision-making power do you have in your family?

    a. more power than any other member of my family

    b. as much power as any other member of my family

    c. less power than most members of my family

    d. less power than any other member of my family

19. How much decision-making power do you have in your working environment? (If not working outside the home at present, use your last job as a basis for answering this question.)

    a. more power than most members of my work team

    b. as much power as any other member of my work team

    c. less power than most members of my work team

    d. less power than any other member of my work team

20. To what extent do you believe that events in your life are merely the result of luck, fate, or chance?

    a. to very little extent

    b. to little extent

    c. to some extent

    d. to a great extent

21. What is your best guess as to the extent and quality of contact you had with your parent(s) shortly after birth?

    a. was given an above average amount of contact by happy parent(s)

    b. was given an average amount of contact by happy parent(s)

    c. was given an average amount of contact by unhappy (perhaps angry) parent(s)

    d. was given a below average amount of contact by unhappy (perhaps angry) parent(s).

22. During your early childhood, to what extent was your mother both calm and generally permissive?

    a. to a very great extent

    b. to some extent

    c. to little extent

    d. to very little extent

23. IIow easily do you make friends in a strange situation?

    a. very easily

    b. easily

    c. uneasily

    d. very uneasily

24. When highly stressed, how likely are you to ask friends or relatives for help?

    a. very likely

    b. likely

    c. unlikely

    d. very unlikely

25. In comparison with other people, how likely are you to see others as threatening, uncooperative, or exploitative?

    a. highly unlikely

    b. unlikely

    c. likely

    d. highly likely

26. How often are you confused about the intentions of others toward you?

    a. very infrequently

    b. infrequently

    c. frequently

    d. very frequently

27. To what extent are you aware of practical, healthy ways of relaxing?

    a. to a very great extent

    b. to some extent

    c. to little extent

    d. to very little extent

28. How frequently do you pursue some highly relaxing practice?

    a. daily or more often

    b. once or twice a week

    c. once or twice a month

    d. seldom

29. How often do you engage in a spiritual practice such as prayer, meditation, or inspirational reading to enrich your interior life?

    a. daily or more often

    b. once or twice a week

    c. once or twice a month

    d. seldom

30. How connected do you feel to your conception of a higher power or to a worthy cause?

    a. to a very great extent

    b. to some extent

    c. to little extent

    d. to very little extent

31. To what extent do you believe your life has purpose?

    a. to a very great extent

   b. to some extent

   c. to little extent

   d. to very little extent

32. How much contact do you have with what you would con-
    sider a spiritual community?

   a. very much

   b. much

   c. very little

   d. none

Scoring Legend

Please note that the scoring legend has been derived rationally,
not empirically. Nevertheless, you might find it interesting to compute your score for each of the scales below using the following legend: "a" = 4; "b" = 3; "c" = 2; "d" = 1.

Wellness Scale (sum of scores for questions 1-7 divided by 7   _____

Thought Control Scale (sum of scores for questions 8-13,
divided by 6   _____

Active Coping Scale (sum of scores for questions 14-20,
divided by 7   _____

Social Ease Scale (sum of Scores for questions 21-26,
divided by 6   _____

Tension Reduction Scale (sum of scores for questions
27-28, divided by 2   _____

Spiritual Practice Scale (sum of scores for questions
29-32, divided by 4   _____

Overall Score (sum of the scale scores above, divide by 6   _____

Interpreting Your Score. A perfect score on each scale would be 4.
With this in mind, we might construct the following interpretive key:

An overall score of 3.5+ suggests you may be a superior stresscoper.

An overall score of 2.5–3.4 suggests you may be an above average
stresscoper.

An overall score of 1.5–2.4 suggests you may be an average
stresscoper.

An overall score of less than 1.5 suggests you may be a below average stresscoper.

In the following sections we discuss four of the six scales appearing on the Stress Coping Resources Inventory: wellness, social ease, tension reduction, and spiritual practice. We suggest that you pay particular attention to any resource on which you gave yourself a below average score on the inventory above. Thought control is discussed fully in chapter 8 and chapter 9. Active coping was discussed in chapter 5.

Wellness: A General Resistance Factor

High-level wellness improves your general resistance to stress by increasing your energy reserves. When you are tired, every task seems stressful. Vince Lombardi would tell his Green Bay Packers, "Fatigue makes cowards of us all." Wellness is a state of good health and high energy. Your wellness score on the Stress Coping Resources Inventory was derived mainly from your answers to questions regarding exercise, rest, and diet.

The difficulty is that achieving wellness requires self-responsibility and self-discipline—attributes often in short supply. We often look for someone or something outside ourselves to save us from unhealthy lifestyles. We bring our bodies to our doctors like we bring our autos to the mechanic and insist, "I brought it; now you fix it!" Donald Ardell (1977) paraphrased John F. Kennedy's admonition when he said, "Ask not what your doctor can do for you, but what you can do for yourself." It seems that we prefer gulping pills and guzzling pharmaceutical potions to exercising a disciplined lifestyle. We need to heed the moral of the story told by the comedian Henny Youngman about a man who prayed to win the lottery. After many prayers and lost lotteries, he heard a booming voice out of the heavens that said, "At least meet me halfway—buy a ticket!" If you hope to enjoy a high level of wellness, you have to buy a ticket—and the ticket is self-discipline. Pursuing high-level wellness can markedly extend your life. Those benefits are demonstrated in the Health Habits and Life Expectancy inventory below.

Health Habits and Life Expectancy

Instructions: Begin your computation with 76 years, which according to the U.S. National Center for Health Statistics (1998), is the average life expectancy in the United States for all races and sexes combined, rounded to the nearest full year. Then, follow the steps below:

If you are a white male, subtract 3 years.

If you are a black male, subtract 11 years.

All other U.S. males, subtract 8 years.

If you are a white female, add 4 years.

If you are a black female, subtract 2 years.

All other U.S. females, subtract 0 years.

If you live in an urban area with a population over 2 million, subtract 2 years.

If you live in a town with a population under 10,000 or on a farm, add 1 year.

If any natural grandparent lived to 85 or more, add 2 years.

If all four natural grandparents lived to 80 or more, add 5 additional years.

If either natural parent died of a stroke or heart attack before the age of 50, subtract 4 years.

If any natural parent, brother, or sister under 50 has (or had) cancer or a heart condition, or has had diabetes since childhood, subtract 3 years.

Do you earn over $100,000 a year? Subtract 1 year.

If you finished college, add 1 year. If you have a graduate or professional degree, add 2 more.

If you are 65 or over and working at something you enjoy, add 2 years.

If you live with a spouse, friend, or family member, add 4 years. If not, subtract 1 year for every ten years alone since age 25, unless you have pets.

If you have strong social ties, add 1 year.

If your work is sedentary, such as sitting at a desk, subtract 2 years.

If your work requires regular physical activity, such as farm or factory labor, add 2 years.

If you exercise regularly and moderately (walking, running, swimming, bicycling, etc.) three to five times a week for at least half an hour (5 minutes warm-up, 20 minutes aerobic activity, 5 minutes cool down), add 4 years.

Do you sleep more than ten hours each night? Subtract 3 years.

If you are intense, aggressive, and easily angered, subtract 2 years.

If you are easygoing, laid back, and peaceful, add 2 years.

Do you have a compelling purpose in life, something important yet to be done? Add 1 year.

Are you happy? Add 1 year.

Unhappy? Subtract 2.

Have you had a speeding ticket in the past year? Subtract 1 year.

If you always wear a seat belt, add 1 year.

Do you smoke more than two packs of cigarettes a day? Subtract 8 years. One or two packs? Subtract 6. One half to one? Subtract 3. If you regularly smoke a pipe or cigars, subtract 2.

If you are a male and have more than 3 drinks a day or more than 21 drinks a week, subtract 2 years. If you are a female and have more than 2 drinks a day or more than 14 drinks a week, subtract 2 years.

Are you overweight by 50 pounds or more? Subtract 8 years. By 30 to 50 pounds? Subtract 4. By 10 to 30 pounds? Subtract 2.

If you feel relaxed and stress-free most of the time, add 1 year. If you feel uptight and under a high degree of stress most of the time, subtract 2.

If you are a male over 40 and have regular physical checkups, add 2 years.

If you are a female over 18 and/or sexually active and you see a gynecologist once a year, add 2 years.

If your diastolic blood pressure (the bottom number) is under 90, add 1 year. If it is from 90 to 104, subtract 1 year. If it is above 104, subtract 2 years.

Age Adjustment

If you are from 32 to 43, add 2 years.

If you are from 44 to 52, add 3 years.

If you are from 53 to 57, add 4 years.

If you are from 58 to 61, add 5 years.

If you are from 62 to 65, add 6 years.

If you are 66 or older, add 7 years.

Source: U.S. National Center for Health Statistics, *Vital Statistics of the United States;* U.S. Bureau of the Census, Statistical Abstract of the United States: 1998, 118th ed. (Washington, D.C.: 1988).

This inventory reminds us that we are constantly making choices that significantly impact how long we will live. Would it surprise you to learn that more than 70,000 Americans are centenarians? With the help of medical research and wellness practices it seems quite likely that many more people will reach such venerable ages. In fact, the U. S. Census Bureau estimates the number of centenarins will reach 834,000 by the year 2050 (Volz 2000). Two wellness practices that can significantly extend our lives are proper exercise and sufficient rest.

Exercise

According to the Health Habits and Life Expectancy inventory, you can add six years to your life expectancy by increasing your activity—that is, by avoiding sedentary work, by choosing work that requires regular physical activity, and by exercising regularly and moderately. We often are short on energy because we are getting too *little* exercise. Most people studiously avoid exercise. If you don't believe it, just watch shoppers in the parking lot drive around for five minutes to get a spot thirty feet closer to the entry. Because the stress response was bred into our ancient ancestors to enable them to fight wild animals, vigorous action is nature's way of getting rid of stress hormones. Any activity will help.

A famous London study of transportation workers found that drivers sitting all day had 66 percent more heart attacks than the conductors who were collecting tickets on double-decker buses. The Institute of Aerobic Research reported that the death rate dropped from 64 to 25.5 per 10,000 when men engaged in moderate amounts of exercise. And in a follow-up study of 17,000 Harvard alumni with ages ranging from 35 to 74, death rates were 25 to 33 percent lower for those who expended at least 2,000 calories per week when compared with less active men (Hayflick 1994). So, look for opportunities to become active. Walk rather than ride; stand rather than sit; climb stairs rather than take the elevator.

Aerobic Exercise

Aerobic exercise is particularly effective in improving wellness. Just look at a few of the many health benefits to be derived from this form of exercise.

- It greatly reduces stress arousal by burning stress hormones.

- It lowers the risk of heart attacks and strokes by raising levels of high-density lipoprotein and lowering low-density lipoprotein, strengthening the heart muscle, and lowering blood pressure.

- It improves immune defenses against infectious diseases and cancer.

- It hardens bone structure, thus decreasing the risk of osteoporosis.

- It increases your energy by building red blood cells and improving the efficiency of mitochondria—factories within cells that produce energy.

- It assists in controlling the appetite.

- It deepens the sleep cycle.

All of these benefits are derived by aerobically exercising only thirty minutes or so a day. *Aerobic* is a word that means oxygen, and aerobic exercise is exercise that allows you to take in approximately the same amount of oxygen that the body is using up during the exercise. A simple way of knowing whether your pace is aerobic is to monitor your heart rate. If your heart rate falls within your aerobic training range, you are aerobically exercising regardless of the activity.

To compute your aerobic training range (ATR), you must first establish your maximum heart rate (MHR). Because your maximum heart rate decreases one beat each year of your life, you must subtract your age from 220, which is the maximum heart rate of infants. Because it would be dangerous to exercise at your MHR, use 60 and 85 percent of your MHR to obtain the lower and upper limits of your ATR. Expressed as formulas, the MHR and ATR would look like this:

MHR: 220 minus Your Age

ATR: (.60 X MHR) to (.85 X MHR)

Thus, if you were forty years old, your MHR would be 180 and your ATR would be 108 to 153.

The good news is that the worse your fitness condition is, the *less* you have to do to get into your training range. If you are in bad enough shape, just standing up may do it! The bad news is if you wish to improve, you must do more. If you are just beginning, set modest goals. Perhaps you may wish to begin by walking one mile or less per day; then, increase the distance as your conditioning improves. Walk four to five minutes and then take your pulse. If your count is within your range, continue on at the same speed. If the count is below the range, speed up slightly. If it is above the range, slow your pace. As long as you are in your training range, time spent is more important than speed.

Many people use aerobic exercise to reduce stress buildup. After a stressful day at work, it is tempting to lie back in the recliner and vegetate in front of the TV. Although this practice is not bad in itself, it is less likely to reduce stress hormones than a short period of exercise. Quite often moderate exercise overcomes your tiredness and blows away stress clouds.

Ah! A Good Night's Sleep

A recent Gallup poll reveals that one of every three Americans suffers from occasional or frequent insomnia. About 9 percent has chronic insomnia, and four of ten insomniacs medicate themselves to get to sleep. The consequences of insomnia range from mild daytime drowsiness to serious injury and death. Moreover, the absence of sleep over time depletes your energy and renders common experiences more stressful.

The Rhythm of Brain Waves

The brain is constantly creating brain waves measured in microvolts. It requires an amplifier, an EEG, to measure them. Basically there are four waves: A feverish *beta* wave that is high in frequency and low in amplitude. The lowest frequency and highest amplitude wave is called *delta*. *Alpha* and *theta* are "in-between" waves. Beta and alpha waves are considered wakeful waves, and when alpha waves are dominant, the muscles are flacid and deeply relaxed. Indeed, there are "alpha trainers," electronic machines that can help people learn to enjoy the relaxation associated with alpha wave dominance. Theta and delta are deep sleep, or coma, waves. When you lie down tonight to go to sleep, it will likely take you fifteen to twenty minutes. Suddenly, you will drop from a mixture of beta and alpha waves to pure alpha waves. This is that point in your sleep cycle where one or more limbs may jerk. Immediately thereafter you fall into sleep. The first ninety minutes or so you spend largely in theta and delta, and then you return to a combination of beta and alpha. The next twenty to thirty minutes you spend dreaming while the brain is kicking out beta and alpha waves once again. You typically cycle between time spent in deep sleep (theta and delta) and dream sleep (beta and alpha). Both deep sleep and dream sleep are vital to your welfare.

Deep Sleep for Recuperation

As you approach delta in deep sleep, the rate at which your cells are burning energy slows down and blood vessels dilate. This deep sleep is valuable for physiological recuperation. The dilated vessels allow the blood to eliminate metabolites that fatigue muscle tissue and cause general nervousness. Moreover, there is an increase in a growth hormone in deep sleep as well (Dement 1999). The growth hormone is not only useful for growth but also for replenishing worn-out body tissues. So, if you sleep deeply during the night you should feel reinvigorated in the morning. Stress often lightens your sleep. People suffering from intense stress may wake in the morning wondering if they were actually asleep at all during the night. Aging also lightens your sleep. Many people over sixty years of age seldom reach delta sleep again, and consequently, their brains release very little growth hormone at night.

Dream Sleep—A Natural De-Stressor

Dream sleep is also vital to your health, not for physiological recuperation but for emotional health and cognitive functioning. During dream sleep your brain engages in three important functions. It partially de-emotionalizes you to the previous day's emotional experiences. Grandma was right when she said, "Sleep on it. It'll be better in the morning." She would have been more correct if she had said, "Dream on it," for it is the dreaming that is the natural de-stressor. Dreaming also is associated with increased memory consolidation. It appears to cross-index memories—taking new experiences and fusing them with older ones, thus making more sense out of them. Have you ever had the experience, while studying a complex body of information at night, where you became so confused that you gave up in despair and went to sleep—only to find that in the morning you understood the information better? The experience is called *reminescence*. You were sleeping, but brain structures were busy sorting out and assigning meaning to your recent experiences. Additionally, dreaming seems to maintain your sense of time and space. In experiments where volunteers were deprived of sleep for many nights, subjects would often begin to lose their grip on reality—their sense of time and space.

Medication and Insomnia

Both deep sleep and dream sleep, then, contribute greatly to our wellness. Stress often disturbs the sleep pattern, endangering either deep sleep, dream sleep, or both. Stress in the form of anxiety often makes it more difficult to fall asleep, and stress in the form of depression often makes it difficult to go back to sleep when you awaken in the night. Prolonged periods of disturbed sleep qualify as forms of insomnia. Unfortunately, some of the "help" we get from pharmaceutical products for insomnia create problems. For example, tricyclic antidepressants, barbiturates, and alcohol all reduce dream sleep. Benzodiazepines, like Valium and Librium, reduce time spent in delta sleep. Caffeine and diet pills delay sleep onset. Alcohol has an initial depressant effect that assists the person to go to sleep, but the depressant effect is followed four hours later with an alerting effect. Overall, sleep preparations tend to increase the length of sleep but may reduce the quality of sleep. In addition, tolerance for some earlier classes of sleeping pills has been a problem. The safety of sleeping pills, however, has improved somewhat over the years. Alcohol and diluted forms of morphine were widely used until the nineteenth century. The barbiturates then reigned until the 1970s, when the benzodiazepines took first place. They were a distinct improvement over the barbiturates, but their effects on the brain were still more general than was desirable. The latest, safest, and currently most prescribed hypnotic medication is zolpidem, with the trade name Ambien. It is much more selective in its effects upon the brain than previous classes of sleeping pills and doesn't cause residual drowsiness the next day (Dement 1999). It is generally considered preferable, however, to deal with insomnia by making changes in your lifestyle rather than depending on hypnotic medications for extended periods.

Fight Insomnia with Carbohydrates

Carbohydrates, whether sugar or starch, tend to make people less active and more calm or sleepy. The secret is tryptophan, an amino acid that increases the production of serotonin, a substance crucial for sleep. Carbohydrates increase tryptophan, which increases serotonin, which increases sleepiness. A carbohydrate snack shortly before bedtime, then, may help you sleep better. High-protein foods such as steak and eggs, however, have the opposite effect. You might want a high-protein lunch to boost alertness and thinking during the afternoon, but late-night snacks should be limited to carbohydrates such as fruits or vegetables.

Do's and Don'ts of Good Sleep

Sometimes our efforts to sleep are counterproductive. You can't *make* yourself go to sleep. The gentle tyrant will take over whenever your stimulation level drops below a certain threshold. Although you can't make yourself go to sleep, you can prepare the conditions for sleep. The following is a list of suggestions for preparing the conditions:

- Don't engage in challenging physical or mental work within two hours of retiring.

- Don't eat, watch TV, or read in bed. You need to associate the bed only with sleep.

- Don't drink alcohol heavily before retiring.

- Don't smoke at all and don't use caffeine late in the evening.

- Do maintain a regular sleep-wake schedule—going to bed at roughly the same hour and rising roughly at the same hour.

- Do reduce light and noise in the room.

- Do sleep in a cool room—approximately 60 degrees.

- Do use a relaxation procedure such as prescribed breathing or deep-muscle relaxation before retiring if you are having trouble getting sleepy.

Develop Social Ease

Our needs are met largely in a social context. Frustrated needs create a great deal of stress. Consequently, social skills and social support networks become effective measures for preventing stress. Social alienation intensifies stressful feelings. The sense that you have nobody with whom you can share your private feelings or have close contact increases your chances of a heart attack by two to five times! At Duke University Redford Williams found that patients with severe coronary heart disease who lacked social support had a death rate three times higher than patients who had a spouse or close friend (Sapolsky 1998). Having a strong social support network across which you can spread the shock of stressful experiences is a powerful coping resource.

The usefulness of the social support network will depend on three things: the scope of the network, its depth, and your willingness to draw upon it. Generally speaking, the depth of the network is more important than its scope. You may have many acquaintances but share intimacy with none of them. A few friends or family members with whom you can bare your soul and who stand ready to share resources with you will be far more valuable in reducing stress than a wide network of shallower relationships. Nevertheless, it is best to have both—a comfortable familiarity with a large number of people *and* a select circle of intimate friends.

Some people are lucky enough to have been born in cohesive families that provide strong social support Others, however, lack such a valuable inheritance. They will have to create such support for themselves. Three sets of social behaviors are useful in creating social support: reaching-out behaviors to establish contact with others, friendship skills to reward others, and assertiveness skills to negotiate with others for the meeting of your needs. If you believe your social network is too thin, try the following behaviors:

1. **Reach out to others.** Try first to increase the number of your contacts. This means you will have to run the risk of being rejected now and then. Fear of rejection is a major barrier to making contact for some people. They choose to remain lonely rather than expose themselves to the possibility of rejection. If you are fearful, run an experiment on a small scale. Choose only one or two people to approach. Choose them carefully to increase the likelihood of gaining a positive reception. Chances are good that your reaching out will be rewarded. Do not expect others to come to you. Place yourself in situations where contacts become possible: Join clubs, attend religious services or other public gatherings, have lunch with fellow employees.

   Once you have increased the scope of your social contacts, select a few people with whom you wish to build intimacy. This form of reaching out will require self-disclosure—sharing feelings and experiences—that involves some risk. Again, if you are fearful, run an experiment.

2. **Practice friendship skills.** You will be more successful in building intimacy if you practice friendship skills. Friendship skills require attending, listening, and reinforcing. *Attend* to others by dropping other activities when others want your attention. Attend to them by making frequent but appropriate contact. Remember them on special occasions. *Listen* with full attention. This requires effort; we usually are entertaining myriad other thoughts while others are talking. If you listen carefully you can often pick up what others are trying to communicate, even if they are having trouble saying it. Such perceptiveness on your part will prove very rewarding to others. Support and reinforce others. Learn the vocabulary of encouragement, and don't be afraid to express your warmth.

3. **Learn to be assertive.** This does not mean being aggressive. Assertiveness is merely the honest expression of what you feel, believe, and want from others *without trying to force them to give it*. Aggressive responses do not take into consideration the costs to yourself and others. In the interest of developing friendship you will often accommodate the wishes of others; however, there will be times in which you believe requests are excessive. In such cases being assertive will require you to say "no." There is no virture in saying "yes" to the manifold requests of others if you can't say "no." Being assertive also involves respecting yourself enough to share your opinions without having to have an airtight logical case for them. It also means being willing to ask for favors from others if you have freely shared your resources with them. There are skillful ways of asserting yourself, and these skills can be learned. With such skills you will gain a freedom of expression without undue cost to yourself or others.

Tension Reduction

Another set of coping resources of immense value in preventing stress are tension-reduction practices. Stress creates tension throughout the body, and chronic tension in turn creates muscular pain and uncomfortable mental states. Practicing forms of relaxation on a daily basis will keep tension from building to dangerous levels. These practices can be performed in a few minutes' time, and they will contribute greatly to the quality of your life. Fortunately, there are many effective practices for relaxing. We have singled out three such practices for special attention. You may increase the effectiveness of all three of these practices by assuming the following posture: Sit in an erect (but not rigid) posture with your eyes closed, your arms loosely resting in your lap, and your lower legs at a ninety-degree angle with your thighs. A straight-back chair with padding but without arms is preferable.

Regulated Breathing

Regulating your breathing is a useful practice in lowering stressful arousal. It may be thought of as an emergency technique, as it can be accomplished within a few minutes. The manner in which you approach a stressful situation will significantly influence the effectiveness of your efforts to cope with it. Many people become anxious in situations such as asking their employer for a raise, confronting a fellow worker, or speaking in public. Their anxiety creates an awkward situation and makes it difficult for them to act effectively. You may find that you can better manage such anxiety if you can begin in a calm manner. You may not have an extended period for preparation, but you can regulate your breathing in less than three minutes.

When stressed, your breathing often loses its natural rhythm. You may over-breathe and veer toward hyperventilation; or you may under-breathe, with apnea-like pauses in air intake that result in a condition known as *hypoxia*. In either case a change in the balance between oxygen and carbon dioxide blood levels is likely. Oxygen contributes to alkalinity within the blood and carbon dioxide contributes to an acid quality. The ratio between the two is expressed as a *pH* value. To sustain life, the pH value must center around 7.40. Dysrhythmic breathing disturbs this critical balance, and people often report feelings of uneasiness from the imbalance. Regulating your breathing is an effective way of restoring the pH balance and creating a calm mental state. To properly regulate your breathing remember the numbers 3-12-6. Take three seconds to breathe in. Hold the breath for twelve seconds, and take three seconds to exhale. Do six cycles of this breathing and experience the increasing calmness that results.

The Quieting Response

The Quieting Response (Stroebel 1978) is another relaxation technique that requires only a few minutes. It leans heavily upon the use of visualization. The following lists the steps involved in the practice.

1. "Alert mind, calm body." (Visualize the muscles throughout your body loosening as you say, "calm body."

2. Smile inwardly.

3. Inhale slowly, imagining that your breath is coming from your feet.

4. Exhale in the same way (breath returning to your feet).

5. Let your shoulders slump.

6. Sense a wave of warmth and heaviness coming over you.

Deep Muscle Relaxation

The stress response causes muscle to contract, and recurring stress creates a condition called *bracing* in which the muscles begin to spasm. A "positive feedback loop" between neurons embedded in muscles and the hypothalamus (a neurostructure) plays a major role in regulating emotions. Once the neurons in the muscles signal the hypothalamus that the muscles are tensing, the hypothalamus triggers emotional reactions that cause further tensing. The practice of deep muscle relaxation is designed to reverse the feedback loop, to relax the muscles, and in the process to evoke mental tranquility. The practice involves the major muscle groups. You first tense a muscle group for seven seconds and then allow it to relax for twenty to thirty seconds before moving on to the next muscle group. Muscles will relax more completely if you first tense them. The following is a list of steps involved.

1. Sit in the same posture used for regulated breathing; that is, in an erect (but not rigid) posture with your eyes closed, your arms loosely resting in you lap, and your lower legs at a ninety-degree angle with your thighs.

2. Extend your arms in front of you and tense your fists to the point of pressure but not of pain. Hold the position for seven seconds. Drop your arms abruptly to your lap and let them rest for twenty to thirty seconds. You will continue alternating tension with relaxation for each of the remaining muscle groups.

3. Next, extend your arms in front of you once again and this time point your fingers to the ceiling as though you were trying to push a wall in front of you. This will tense your wrist and lower forearm muscles.

4. Touch the tops of your shoulders with the tips of your fingers to tense the bicep muscles.

5. Now begin with the muscles running under the skin in the head area. If you are not wearing contact lens, shut your eyes tightly. This will tense the muscles in the scalp, forehead, and around the sockets of the eyes.

6. Push the tongue into the top of your mouth, clinch your molar teeth together, and pull the corners of your lips around toward your ears.

7. Push the head down about one inch off the sternum bone at the same time and attempt to pull the head back. This will tense the huge muscles in the back of your neck.

8. Take a deep breath and hunch the shoulders up toward the ears. This will tense the shoulder and upper back muscles.

9. Take another deep breath and this time attempt to touch the shoulders together in the back.

10. Now suck in the stomach, in tensing the abdominal muscles.

11. Scrunch your rear end into your chair, tensing the buttocks muscles.

12. Lift your heels about six inches off the floor while you extend your legs. Feel the tension in the thigh muscles.

13. Lift your heels and extend your legs again, this time pointing the toes toward the knees, stretching the calf muscles and tensing the shin muscles.

14. Lift your heels and extend your legs a third time. This time curl your toes under toward your arches. Tense the arch muscle only three seconds or you may produce cramping in the arches.

15. At this point sit quietly for one minute or so.

16. Now, use the powers of your imagination to further relax your muscles. Focus on one muscle group after another and visualize the muscles spreading out, getting long, loose, and more and more deeply relaxed. Imagine the muscle fibers to be like wet spaghetti and all the muscles becoming like Jell-O. Sit quietly for an additional period of healing silence while soaking up those feelings of deep muscle relaxation.

Strengthen Your Spiritual Practice

A spiritual worldview gives you the feeling that life has meaning. The word *spiritual* is used to mean many different things. Many persons immediately think of organized religion when the word *spiritual* is mentioned. Indeed, most people pursue their spiritual development through religion. Others, however, pursue their spiritual development outside of formal, institutionalized religion. Whether inside or outside of formal religion, spirituality gives you the feeling of being connected to "Something" that is larger and more important than your narrow sense of ego.

The "Something" may be thought of as a supreme being, the life force, creative evolution, the human family, or a cause such as world peace. God, the Ultimate, the Ground of Being, *élan vital*, "the Force" (in George Lucas's *Star Wars* saga), the Tao, Krishna, Brahma, Allah, Buddha, Higher Power—many names are used to refer to the "Something." In every case, however, they refer to the ultimate good in the universe. In some traditions the "Something" is thought of as being largely transcendent, that is, outside of human experience. In other traditions it is said to be immanent, that is, dwelling within us.

Herbert Benson, Harvard professor, teamed up with Jared Kass, an experienced meditator in the Conservative Jewish tradition, to construct the INSPIRIT scale, a measure of spirituality (1984). The scale measures the feeling that there is *more than just me.* They discovered that this feeling was not necessarily religious in the traditional sense and that high scores on the scale were related to better psychological health. In a study of 1,473 Americans, researchers found that those who did not participate in spiritual practice were more than twice as likely to report health problems than those who did. In addition, members of more liberal religious groups enjoyed better health than those in more conservative groups (Brown 1993).

Increased Self-Awareness

Spiritual practice most often leads to increased self-awareness. Self-awareness does not mean self-consciousness. Self-consciousness is fearful preoccupation with oneself stemming from a lack of self-respect and self-confidence. When self-conscious people confront challenging situations, they feel threatened and their attention turns to inward damage control. They give themselves a vote of "no confidence" and worry so much about failure that they have little attention and energy to devote to the task at hand. Their anticipation of failure becomes a self-fulfilling prophecy.

Self-awareness, on the other hand, is a matter of recognizing what you are doing and why you are doing it *while* you are doing it. This awareness brings freedom. Self-awareness is accompanied by self-respect and self-confidence. Whereas self-awareness breeds self-love, self-consciousness breeds selfishness. When you are a problem to yourself, you become self-preoccupied and consequently, you are less considerate of others. Most spiritual disciplines are designed to increase one's self-awareness. Meditation, yoga, prayer, and similar approaches for increasing self-awareness will be discussed in detail in chapter 12.

Expanded Self-Identity

Spiritual practice also leads to an expanded self-identity. The sense of connectedness with a force larger than yourself frees you from ego encapsulation. Energy is freed up from the defense of the ego and made available for higher pursuits. Just as the socialization process teaches children to learn to share and to become considerate of others, spiritual practice moves you from a narrow preoccupation with your ego interests to a greater concern for the welfare of others.

The mystic Ken Wilber (1996), in *A Brief History of Everything*, suggests that the direction of spiritual development is from an ego-centric, to a socio-centric, to a world-centric, or ecological, view of reality. Moving in this direction, your allegiance expands from self-interest, to family or tribal interests, to an interest in the welfare of humans, other sentient beings, and the environment. An expanded consciousness, with its greater sense of connectedness, removes the fear and stress that comes from alienation, the feeling of being in it alone. Scott Peck, author of *The Different Drum* (1987), like J. Fowler (1981) before him, described spiritual development as occurring in stages. With each advancing stage your sense of identity becomes ever more inclusive of others.

Stage One

This is a stage of undisciplined spirituality referred to as chaotic and antisocial. People stuck at this stage are governed purely by their own wills without respect to the interests of others. Their awareness is trapped within their own egoistic desires, and they lack empathy for others. This is the stage of children and a small number of adults who are fixated in their spiritual development.

Stage Two

In this stage the person is rigidly conforming to formal, institutionalized religious prescriptions. The person does not challenge the official dogma or the traditions of the group, and others at this stage of development would not condone such challenges if they were offered. Theirs is a blind allegiance to the letter of the law.

Stage Three

At this stage of spiritual development people feel free to interpret religious teachings and practices according to their understanding.

They are not iconoclastic; that is, they are not intent on destroying the faith of others. They merely recognize that "official dogma" represents the interpretations of others from the past, and they trust their own intelligence and motivation enough to reinterpret religious prescriptions based on their own experience.

Stage Four

In this, the highest stage of spirituality, persons have moved beyond the narrowness of their religious tradition and embrace other persons coming out of other religious traditions as well. They understand that religious traditions represent the cumulative wisdom of a people at a point in time, that these traditions with their rituals are merely fingers pointing to the Ultimate. They understand that the Ultimate, the Force, God cannot be fully comprehended and that words are totally inadequate to describe this creative force. As Lao Tsu wrote in the first chapter of the *Tao Te Ching*, "The Tao that can be named is not the eternal Tao. The name that can be named is not the eternal name." People who reach stage four are willing to accept the mystery and to honor other interpretations of It as honest, but groping, efforts to grasp Its essence. This understanding leaves them respectful of other interpretations. Their approach, therefore, is *inclusive* rather than exclusive. If they remain active in their religious communities, they accept the practices of their faith as vehicles for transcending the narrowness of their egos and for embracing life. They realize that their commitment to their worldview cannot be empirically proven that they have arrived at such understanding partly through intuition, partly through faith. This does not mean that their spiritual understanding is irrational. It is merely *a*rational. It doesn't fly in the face of science or rationality; it merely transcends them. It delves in the realm of values, and science can only make statements of fact. It incorporates the legacy of science but offers hypotheses regarding reality that go beyond the facts of scientific investigation.

Spirituality, thus, creates a rich interior life—the development of interests that transcend the busyness of our lives. Mindless busyness interferes with the development of spirituality—indeed, busyness may be a vehicle for keeping us from the hard work necessary for spiritual growth. We may emphasize *doing* to the exclusion of *being*. One way to feel intrinsically more valuable and to fight the drivenness of "Type A" behavior is to spend more time *becoming*—becoming an interesting conversationalist, becoming a person with finely honed cultural tastes, becoming an informed person, becoming a person of depth.

Beginning a Spiritual Practice

If you are not presently following a spiritual path, certain publications may assist you in your choice of a discipline. Any effort to assemble all the useful publications for this purpose would require encyclopedic treatment. We would like to recommend three volumes that may prove especially helpful. Hunter Lewis (1990), in *A Question of Values*, reviews the six ways that we go about establishing values in our lives. He presents a brilliant discussion of the use of authority, logic, sense experience, emotion, intuition, and science in arriving at value statements and offers interesting historical examples of how each has been used. Dick Anthony, Bruce Ecker, and Ken Wilber (1987), in *Spiritual Choices*, offer a set of criteria by which you can judge the merits of a spiritual practice. And Huston Smith (1987), in his epochal volume, *The Religions of Man*, presents a respectful and highly readable review of the world's great religions.

We have discussed behaviors here that are highly useful in preventing stress. To review, being sensitive to the early signs of stress buildup offers lead-time for taking action before the situation worsens. This means scanning the body for stressful sensations. A great deal of stress can be prevented by spacing life events and pacing your efforts so as to keep the demand load within an optimal stimulation range. Stress can be prevented by wise decision-making, by avoiding needless ego battles with others, and by learning less confrontational ways of expressing yourself. Because life demands turn into stressors only when we perceive our coping resources as inadequate to deal with them, building additional coping resources is an important way of preventing stress. We have discussed the importance of pursuing high-level wellness to ensure adequate energy, of developing social skills to bring about more ease in the presence of others, to learn and practice relaxation skills, and to increase your sense of spirituality. In the next chapter we examine stress-inducing personalities and suggest ways of neutralizing their hurtfulness.

Chapter 7

Altering Stress-Inducing Personalities

It's much more important to know what sort of person has a disease than what sort of disease the person has.

—Parry of Bath
(sixteenth-century British physician)

There is no illness apart from the mind.

—Hippocrates, 404 B.C.

Like the early English physician, Parry of Bath, physicians for ages have noted the relationship between personality and illness. Sir William

Osler, a famous Canadian physician, remarked at the turn of the twentieth century, "The care of tuberculosis depends more on what the patient has in his head than what he has in his chest." Early on, such beliefs were supported only by anecdotal evidence—physicians casually noting that certain illnesses seemed to be experienced by persons possessing certain personality traits. Over the past few decades, however, systematic research has documented the relationship between the mind and the body. By this time it should come as no surprise that the mediating variable between personality and illness appears to be stress. In other words, certain personality types appear to be stress-inducing and, therefore, associated with ruptured interpersonal relationships, fatigue, unpleasant emotions, and higher rates of illness and even death.

The purpose of this chapter is to acquaint you with some of the more troublesome personality styles that can contribute to stress. *Personality* is a word in common use, but psychologists define it as a cluster of traits that account for the unique and relatively consistent ways that each of us feels and behaves. When reading about the personality styles reviewed here, you may see a little of yourself in each one. The traits that make up these personalities are quite common. But taken to an extreme, each of these personalities can contribute greatly to the stress an individual experiences.

Why Is Everyone So Cranky?

C. Leslie Charles (1999) came up with a quick, and unpopular answer to the question, "Why is everyone so cranky?": Look in the mirror! Although she readily acknowledged the myriad stresses that are a part of modern life, she emphasizes the control we have over our reactions to these events. And the people that she describes as "cranky" approach everyday life with a set of attitudes that nearly guarantees dissatisfaction. These attitudes include:

- The belief that you not only have the right to pursue happiness, but also that you *deserve* happiness and that you have the right to go to any length to achieve it;

- The belief that your emergencies take precedence over anyone else's emergencies; and

- The belief that you are entitled to what you want when you want it.

These self-centered beliefs create a great deal of unnecessary stress. Your beliefs influence your perceptions of what is happening; and your perceptions largely determine your emotional reactions.

Insane reactions such as "road rage" accordingly are the direct result of individuals who allow themselves to become hyper-stressed about events which are inevitable in modern society. If you choose to live in a large metropolitan area and use the roads at peak times of the day, it should come as no surprise that you will encounter traffic jams. In fact, C. Leslie Charles says, one should *plan* for it so that frustrations don't boil over into regrettable actions.

For example, Chris currently drops off his daughter at middle school on the way to work in the morning and lands in the middle of peak commuter traffic. Although he normally despises sitting in stop-and-go traffic, he decided somewhere near the beginning of the school year to make this trip a happy part of his day. He realized that this was a time when he could talk with his daughter Colleen without distractions such as the phone or television. He makes sure to bring his commuter mug of tea along, as well as his dental floss (per Colleen's request, he waits to floss until after he drops her off). This potentially stressful event becomes tolerable because he not only expects it to happen, he plans for it. Sounds simple, doesn't it? But many people still end up getting extremely stressed out when encountering traffic jams, long waits at the doctor's office, or crowds at shopping malls.

It is important to understand to what extent your response to a stressor is determined by the situation itself and to what extent by enduring mental habits. Examining this issue, Susan Folkman and Richard Lazarus (1980) reported finding little consistency in people's coping responses across different stressful situations. They maintained that the influence of stressful circumstances upon coping is so strong that it overpowers the influence of personality traits. If this were so, then the concept of personality as a predisposer of stress would be misleading. However, other researchers (Ben-Porath and Tellegen 1990; Krohne 1990; Watson 1990) have challenged Folkman and Lazarus's conclusion, emphasizing instead the role that personality traits play in influencing the choice of coping methods. These researchers point out that personality traits *do* interact with the situation in shaping perceptions of stress. Moreover, it appears that the effect of threatening life situations actually is to accentuate preexisting traits, and that our true dispositions are best revealed under stress.

Personality: A Link to Recovery from Cardiac Surgery

The influence of personality traits on survival was clearly demonstrated in research conducted at the Rochester School of Medicine in

New York. Several years ago, Dr. Chase Patterson Kimball and his colleagues, all cardiac surgeons, noted that patients undergoing heart surgery had different outcomes depending on their basic attitudes. To investigate this observation more carefully the surgeons enlisted the help of psychologists. The psychologists interviewed fifty-five patients awaiting heart surgery and placed them in one of four groups: *adjusted, symbiotic, denying,* and *depressed.* The adjusted group consisted of thirteen patients who were aware of the dangers of surgery and yet were hopeful that the procedure might improve the quality and extend the length of their lives. They would talk openly and realistically about their approaching surgery with family members and friends.

A second group of fifteen made up the symbiotic group. In biology, *symbiosis* refers to the cooperation of two life forms for their mutual benefit. For example, elephants furnish birds with a food source in the form of insects on their backs, and birds in exchange remove the irritating insects. It is a win-win arrangement. The psychologists concluded that this group of patients did not appear to want to get either better or worse from the operation. They appeared to be deriving rewards from their illness. In some cases family members are more powerful sick than well. These patients had been pressured to have the operation, but at some level of consciousness they recognized that getting well would threaten their position within the family. They appeared to be feeding on their own illness.

A third group of twelve denied feeling any anxiety regarding the surgery. They appeared flippant about the upcoming operation, saying things like, "I'm going to give those doctors and nurses a hard time." Their macho expressions, however, sounded tinny and strained. A fourth group of fifteen were diagnosed as depressed. These were the people who were used to saying, "Why me?"

The results of the operation were tabulated at three and fifteen months after the operations. Table 7-1 presents the results of the follow-up evaluations. There was an astounding relationship between the results of the surgery and group membership. The results are seen to be progressively worse as one comes across the table from the adjusted group to the depressed group. Of the thirteen members in the adjusted group three were unchanged in regard to their illness, nine were improved, none became worse, and one died. Of the fifteen members of the *depressed* group, two were unchanged, one improved, one was judged to be worse, and eleven died! Very simply, adjusted patients had a one in thirteen chance of dying from the cardiac surgery whereas depressed patients had an 11 in 15 chance of dying!

We can see from this research that personality may indeed play an important role in how we cope with stress. And over the past few decades, several personality types have been identified as stress- and disease-inducing. Among them are the *disease-prone personality*, the *carcinogenic personality*, the *thrill-seeking personality*, the *anxious-reactive personality*, and the coronary prone personality (Type A). Each of these areas of research holds potentially valuable insights into the relationship between personality and stress, and we will discuss each in turn.

	Adjusted	Symbiotic	Denying Anxiety	Depressed
Number of Patients	13	15	12	13
Unchanged	3	8	3	2
Improved	9	1	3	1
Worse	0	5	2	1
Dead	1	1	4	11

Table 7-1. Effect of attitude on open-heart surgery.
Source: Chase Patterson Kimball, Rochester School of Medicine

The Disease-Prone Personality

Friedman and Booth-Kewley (1987) conducted a meta-analytic review of 101 research studies that examined the relationship between specific emotions and five diseases with so-called "psychosomatic" components—asthma, arthritis, ulcers, headaches, and coronary heart disease. There was only weak support for the idea that a specific emotion predisposes a person to a specific disease, but the results pointed to the probable existence of a generic disease-prone personality that involves depression, anger/hostility, anxiety, and possibly other aspects of personality. When powerful emotions are mishandled, it seems they may incline the person toward illness in general. Perhaps, then, hereditary weakness or environmental conditions are responsible for the specific health problem that develops.

The Carcinogenic Personality

Many physicians have noted that a disproportionate number of cancer patients were people who seemed to live their lives in an *emotional crouch*—defending themselves against feelings of helplessness and hopelessness. They tended to repress their anger but accept their depression, ignore their achievements but embrace their failures.

In 1958 a group of doctors in the Chicago area evaluated more than 2,000 middle-aged men for signs of depression and other emotional disorders and followed them for the next seventeen years. After other risk factors, such as cigarette smoking, had been controlled, the men who from the beginning had been diagnosed as depressed had a death rate from cancer twice as high as the rate found in the general population. The doctors concluded that depression alone was the precipitating factor.

In the early 1950s doctors at a university hospital conducted a study on forty women entering the hospital to undergo biopsies for breast lumps. They were screened for "hopelessness potential" with a psychological scale that measures how much control people feel over their lives, futures, and the state of their health. Based on this assessment, the doctors predicted which of the forty women would be found to have malignancies. When the biopsy results were studied, the researchers were right in thirty-one of their forty predictions.

The Harvard medical school professor W. W. Meisner et al. (1977) found cancer patients to be "selfless" individuals who are known for making sacrifices and for being self-effacing. Once again, the "hopelessness" and "helplessness" of these patients was noted. Many researchers have drawn attention to the poor self-concepts of cancer patients. Bernie Siegel (1986) noted that such people often see themselves as stupid, clumsy, weak, and inept, even though others may be envious of their achievements. Lawrence LeShan (1977) concluded from his studies that cancer-prone individuals held extremely poor self-expectations coupled with self-dislike. The husband and wife researchers Carl and Stephanie Simonton (1975) noted that cancer patients who were optimistic and held the conviction that they could win over the cancer were more likely to survive the illness.

Both retrospective and prospective studies reveal that the tendency to suppress negative emotions and to be unassertive and docile is correlated with a greater likelihood of developing cancer (Temoshock and Dreher 1992). In a study of 1,350 Yugoslavian residents, researchers were 93 percent accurate in predicting which residents would develop cancer based upon their scores ten years earlier on an eleven-item measure of emotional expressiveness. Of the 166 who had died of cancer over the ten-year period, 158 had answered ten or eleven of the eleven items in a manner that suggested they were throttling their emotions (Grossarth-Maticek, Bastiaans, Kanazir 1985).

You may question whether the gross self-devaluation, helplessness, and hopelessness seen in many cancer patients precedes the illness or is a result of it. It could be that the word *cancer* has such a fatal ring to it that otherwise strong, confident people experience significant personality transformation when diagnosed with it. Certainly, there must be some debilitating effect of the diagnosis, but considerable research seems to suggest that passive, self-deprecating views may to a significant degree predispose the person to the disease.

The Thrill-Seeking Personality

Take a moment to look at the list of descriptors below. Think about the ideal way you would like to lead your life, and then decide to what extent you would rather your life be characteritized by the descriptors in columns A or B.

A	B
Novel	Familiar
Complex	Simple
High-Risk	Low-Risk
High-Conflict	Low-Conflict
Much Variety	Little Variety
High-Intensity	Low-Intensity

According to psychologist Frank Farley (1986), if your preferences were mostly toward the adjectives in column A, you may have what he describes as a "Type T Personality." Although most of us seem to like our thrills in moderation, Farley believes that some individuals possess a cluster of personality traits which predispose them to thrill-seeking, adventure, and high levels of stimulation (the T stands for thrill-seeking). If you prefer mainly the adjectives in column B, you might be one of the people that Farley describes as "little t personalities." Little t's are people who carefully avoid change and excitement and cling tightly to routine. Farley's research led him to conclude that while a significant subset of the population falls into one of these two extreme categories, most of us are somewhere in the middle, preferring neither excessive excitement nor unremitting routine.

Interestingly, thrill-seeking Type T's come in several varieties. Farley subdivides the Type T personality into those who seek this stimulation mainly in mental activities or physical activities. In addition, Farley believes that some Type T's will direct their energies toward creative, socially useful activities in either realm, mental or physical, while others may choose destructive, even criminal, outlets. Figure 7-2 provides an overview of each type.

Type T Personality

Constructive	Destructive

Mental

People who seek prosocial stimulation in intellectual activities such as artists or scientists

Mental

People who seek antisocial stimulation in the mental domain, such as con artists

Physical

People who seek prosocial stimulation in the physical domain, such as adventurers and explorers

Physical

People who seek antisocial stimulation in physical activities such as violent criminals

Figure 7-2. Subtypes of the Type T Personality.

Farley believes that whether you are a Big T or little t, and whether you choose socially appropriate or destructive outlets, are shaped both by genetic predisposition and by your environment when young. Either way, it may be important to know where you fall on the Type T continuum. Because each of us will seek to maintain an optimal level of arousal, optimal stimulation will be influenced by sensitivity to arousal. As we will explain more fully in the following chapter, the *reticular activating system* (RAS) determines whether incoming stimulation will arouse the brain enough to take note. There seem to be significant differences in the sensitivity of people's RAS to stimulation. People who are Type T may be born with, or develop, an RAS that has a high threshold for stimulation; consequently, they need high levels of mental and physical stimulation to reach an optimal level of arousal. In contrast, little t's may be overly responsive to stimulation and thus need very little excitement in their lives to reach this optimal stimulation level.

Biology and Sensation-Seeking

Farley's research on Type T's provides fascinating information on the connection between thrill-seeking and personality, and numerous other researchers, most notable Marvin Zuckerman at the University of Delaware and Monte Buchsbaum at the National Institutes of Health, have searched for similar biological links with what they call sensation-seeking. This research dates back to the early 1900s when Ivan Pavlov noted differences among dogs in regard to their preference for sensation-seeking. One group of dogs was energetic, exploratory, and friendly toward humans, while a second group was cautious in approaching new situations and inhibited around people. In the following decades further efforts were made to discover the relationship between biology and sensation-seeking, and some of these relationship are discussed below.

Characteristics of Sensation Seeking

Zuckerman, Buchsbaum, and Murphy (1980) noted in their studies with college students that those who scored high on the trait of sensation-seeking had a greater tendency to use illegal drugs and cigarettes, to volunteer for unusual kinds of experiments such as sensory deprivation or hypnosis, and to engage in physically dangerous activities such as parachuting or motorcycle riding.

Zuckerman et al. (1980) also identified a considerable body of research linking sensation-seeking to various aspects of physiology. For example, sensation-seekers show greater strength in the "initial orienting reflex" (IOR). The IOR is a type of reflex that includes increased cortical arousal in the brain, changes in activity in the autonomic system, alteration in muscle activity (the halting of other organized activities), and increased sensitivity to light and sound. The IOR is different from a defensive reaction, such as flinching, or a startle reaction because it involves turning *toward* the source of stimulation with subjective feelings of interest and excitement.

These researchers also found sensation-seekers to differ from nonsensation-seekers in regard to the brain's potential for responding to stimuli. The brains of nonsensation-seekers tend to reduce the potential for response while the brains of sensation-seekers tend to increase such potentials. Zuckerman et al. also reported differences between sensation-seekers and non–sensation-seekers in the levels of the enzyme MAO in the brain and levels of the gonadal hormones androgen and estrogen.

Living with Tendencies Toward Thrill- or Sensation-Seeking

So what can we learn from research on thrill- or sensation-seeking? First, it seems important to recognize your optimal stimulation level and make adjustments accordingly. Each of us has a different tolerance for activity and change, and what may be sheer boredom to one individual could be an overdose of excitement for another. As we noted in chapter 3, the accelerating pace of modern life may be ideally tailored to Type T's, but overwhelming to little t's.

Farley (1986) suggests that the United States may be a "Type T nation." Most of our cultural values seem to revolve around the concept of rugged individualism, an idea that seems compatible with a Type T approach to life. We idealize the original colonists who left the shores of Europe, the settlers who moved west in the centuries that followed, and the cowboys and marshalls who roamed the Wild West in their wake. Even today, we are infatuated with professional athletes, successful entrepreneurs, and charismatic leaders who take great risks to achieve individual glory. Such individuals are often held up as role models for others, but it may be that such people represent a unique personality type whose optimal stimulation would be maddening to little t's. It also seems important to note that while many Type T's accomplish positive things, other T's pursue goals that are antisocial and destructive (see Figure 7-2). Therefore, we must be cautious in extolling the virtues of the Type T lifestyle.

Your "T-score" may also have implications for your social relationships, educational environments, and work. Farley found that Type T's tend to be attracted to each other, although the findings in this area are a bit mixed. Not surprisingly, in the educational arena Type T's prefer methods of instruction that are variably paced, interactive, and provided by a dramatic and extroverted teacher. In contrast, little t's may prefer less variety and more structure in the classroom. Finally, and perhaps most obviously, your preference for thrill-seeking can influence your work satisfaction. Although very few Type T's will be able to find employment as professional athletes or stunt drivers, they may still be happier in work environments that offer constant change and interaction with others. Little t's, on the other hand, will likely be happiest in a more routinized, structured environment.

The Anxious-Reactive Personality

Imagine that you have to give an important speech to a crowd of strangers. You have researched your subject thoroughly, have prepared your speaking notes carefully, and have practiced what you want to say several times. However, as the moment of truth draws nearer, you begin to notice your mouth is a little dry. Your heart begins beating a bit faster, and you notice that your palms are a bit sweaty. "Uh-oh," you tell yourself, "I'm starting to flip out. I thought I was ready, but I'm getting more and more anxious every minute. I wanted to come across as a cool customer, but I'll be lucky if I make it through my notes without having a heart attack. Why does this happen to me every time I have to make a presentation?" You go on to survive the ordeal but realize you could have done far better if only you hadn't stressed out so much. The rest of the day will be spent in self-recrimination and self-blame.

Girdano, Everly, and Dusek (1997) have described a personality type, exemplified above, that takes an abnormally long time to recover from stressful stimulation. The dynamics of this adjustment create a self-perpetuating reaction that keeps the stress alive long after the stressor is gone. Because it is primarily the duration rather than the intensity of the stressor that creates long-range damage, anxious-reactive types are particularly prone to chronic psychosomatic disorders. The problem seems to involve a positive feedback system. The person becomes stressed over becoming stressed! The arousal response itself takes on the role of a stressor. This succession of events is depicted in Figure 7-3.

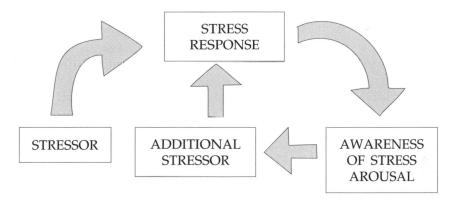

Figure 7-3. Feed forward process of the anxious-reactive personality.

With anxious-reactives, a type of "feed forward" process is set up. Stressors trigger the stress response. The person develops an awareness of the sensations of stressful arousal, and the awareness, itself, becomes a stressor to further arouse the person. Consequently, the process becomes self-perpetuating. One is reminded of Franklin D. Roosevelt's famous dictum, "The only thing we have to fear is fear itself."

Although the muscles send feedback messages that help to perpetuate the stress response, it is the cognitive messages of anxious-reactive personalities that seem the most powerful. When anxious-reactives notice stressful sensations such as trembling hands, cracking voice, or irregular breathing, they may begin a series of self-defeating thoughts such as, "Why do I let myself in for situations like this? I should have known I couldn't handle it!" They may exaggerate the seriousness of the situation and/or discount their resources for handling it. Such people often engage in *catastrophizing*, that is, in their minds every difficult situation is a catastrophe waiting to happen. Thus, anxious-reactive personalities worsen each stressful situation in two ways: first, by using their own anxious cues as stressors, and second, by exaggerating the seriousness of demands and minimizing their ability to cope with them.

The hypersensitivity of anxious-reactive personalities to stressors causes them to require more time in which to lower their arousal. Figure 7-4 depicts the greater recovery time needed by such personalities in comparison with experienced meditators and normal people. In this research, a baseline of arousal is established for normals, meditators, and anxious-reactive personalities. A shrill, unexpected noise is then sounded. Members of all three groups experience the same physiological arousal. The arousal of members of all three groups then begins to return to baseline arousal. Note from Figure 7-4 that the time required for meditators to return to baseline arousal is much shorter than the recovery time for normals. Meditators experienced the same heightened arousal that normals experienced, but the unpleasant noise did not cost them as much. They are no less alert and responsive to the world than the average person, but their stress arousal is shorter-lived. Note particularly the extended recovery time for the anxious-reactive personalities. Their arousal begins to diminish in the same way the arousal of the other

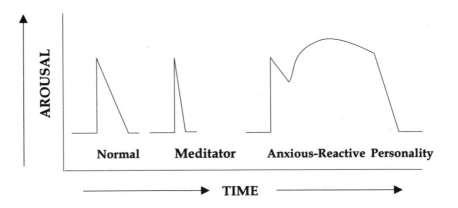

Figure 7-4. Recovery time of normals, meditators, and anxious-reactive personalies.

two groups does, but it suddenly builds once again. It is at this point that their anxious sensations and their catastrophizing trigger further arousal.

Adjusting your Anxious-Reactive Personality

There are two approaches to the treatment of the anxious-reactive personality. First, you must become aware of the self-perpetuating nature of the cycle. You must learn that you are interpreting your anxious sensations as signs of impending doom. You must learn to interpret these sensations as mere conditioned reactions that have no ability to predict future behaviors. In chapter 1 we learned that the damage comes when we jump from sensations to emotions. Emotional reactions stem from interpretations of sensations. The public speaker could interpret her arousal as an energized condition and conclude, "I'm really up for this presentation." Or she could interpret it as nervousness and conclude, "Oh, no! I'm really getting nervous now. I can't function when I'm so scared." According to the the principles of *stress inoculation* (a technique we will discuss in detail later), you must reinterpret the sensations not as harbingers of doom, but as cues to prepare for the challenging situation. These cues are friends, for they signal the upcoming challenge and give you lead time for preparing.

The second approach to the treatment of the anxious-reactive personality is the elimination of the tendencies to catastrophize and to relive stressful experiences from the past. Anxious-reactives exaggerate the seriousness of present demands and process unpleasant experiences over and over again. They can't seem to let go of these unpleasant experiences and move on to a fuller experience of the present. To overcome their hyper-reactivity to stressors, they must become aware of the pattern of their responding. Once they realize that they are ensuring a lifetime of distress by their thinking habits, they must challenge them on every occasion.

Coronary-Prone Personality

Perhaps one of the most disastrous consequences of stress is its potentially destructive effect on the cardiovascular system. The observation that stressful emotions predispose people to heart disease goes back at least a few centuries. In the seventeenth century, William Harvey wrote, "Every affection of the mind that is attended with either pain or pleasure, hope or fear, is the cause of an agitation whose influence extends to the heart ("Stress," 1992, p. 104)." And early in the twentieth century the Canadian physician William Osler wrote, "I believe that the high pressure at which men live, and the habit of working the machine to its maximum capacity, are responsible for arterial degeneration (1910, p. 840)." However, attention to this relationship really took off in the latter half of the century as life expectancies increased from forty-seven years on average to more than 75 years by the year 2000. People were living long enough for the harmful effect of stress on the heart to finally be recognized.

The granddaddy of all the stress-inducing personalities is the coronary prone personality. Such individuals have been described as having a Type A behavior pattern. According to Friedman and Rosenman (1974), the discoverers of this personality type, there are two beliefs underlying the adjustment of Type A's. First, they believe that they are not natively worth much, that their value comes solely from their productions. And second, they believe that whatever success they have had is a result of being able to do more than others in less time. Consequently, coronary-prone individuals suffer from hurry sickness, that is, from the need to do more and more in less and less time. They are constantly racing the clock in an effort to produce. Consequently, when they are not getting things done, they begin to feel worthless. To avoid feelings of worthlessness they maintain a constant backlog of tasks and fill every hour with activity.

Type A Personality Characteristics

Friedman and Rosenman define the Type A behavior pattern as "an action-emotion complex that can be observed in any person who is aggressively involved in a chronic, incessant struggle to achieve more and more in less and less time, and, if required to do so, against the opposing efforts of other things or persons (p. 19)." Because they try to do more than others in less time, they are particularly vulnerable to frustration; and because frustration leads naturally to hostility, Type A individuals experience more hostility than others.

Glass, Contrada, and Snow (1980) noted that Type A individuals strive harder to succeed than do Type B's. In one study they found that Type A's attempted to solve a greater number of arithmetic problems than Type B's, even in the absence of time limits. They also worked at a level closer to the limits of their endurance on a treadmill test than Type B's while admitting to less fatigue. Although they have a greater number of psychosomatic symptoms, they complain less about their symptoms than others. Because of their hurry sickness, they perceive time as passing more quickly than it actually does. They often are amazed at how quickly the hands on the clock move, and they often fault themselves for not being able to accomplish more within a given period of time.

Type A Pattern and Coronary Artery Disease

Type A characteristics appear to predispose you to coronary artery disease. Friedman and Rosenman (1974) maintain that Type A's have a 66 percent greater chance of having a heart attack than their Type B counterparts. The Western Collaborative Studies in San Francisco found that 72 to 85 percent of the 3,411 heart attack victims studied clearly demonstrated the Type A behavior syndrome *before* the onset of their heart attack. The competitiveness, impatience, hostility, and aggressiveness of Type A's keep them in a chronic state of arousal, contributing to the development of coronary artery disease (CAD). The seriousness of the this risk is fully appreciated when you consider that heart disease is the number-one killer in America and that a large percentage of cardiac deaths occur between the ages of 35 and 50 (American Heart Association 1996).

Assessing Your Type A Behaviors

Below is a listing of some of the behaviors that accompany a Type A's "hurry sickness." Read carefully each of these behaviors and honestly judge whether or not the behavior is characteristic of your own personality.

1. **Hurried speech.** Because Type A's feel pressure from the need to justify their worthwhileness by constantly producing, they tend to talk rapidly. Because they have so many back-logged tasks, they may become impatient with the rate of their own speech and react by finishing their sentences quicker than they begin them. Their impatience may result in explosive accentuation of words without any logical connection to the content. Moreover, they may become bored with what they are saying because their tongues can't keep up with their racing thoughts, and they may go on to the next thought before finishing the last one.

   Behavior is ____ or is not ____ characteristic of me.

2. **Rapid movement and rapid eating.** Suffering from "hurry sickness," Type A's may jerk about like a water bug on a pond. When they eat, they may gulp down the food like a hound dog. Such persons usually finish an entire meal before their companions are through with the appetizer.

Onlookers may be prompted to look under the table to see if they are passing food to a hound dog. Such individuals seem to be awaiting the day when food comes out in pill form.

Behavior is ____ or is not ___ characteristic of me.

3. **Thinking and performing several things at once.** Type A's seldom are concentrated on doing one thing at a time. Rather, while doing one thing, they may be thinking about five other things that need attention. Because of the pressure they feel from the litany of tasks they have taken on, they may engage in *polyphasic behavior*, that is, doing several things at once. If they are interviewing someone in their office, they may "make their time count" by filling out a travel voucher or sorting through the morning's mail. If they are driving home, they may continue making telephone calls on their cell phones. If in the evening their spouses engage them in conversation, they can sandwich in other interests by turning on the TV and placing the newspaper in their laps at the same time.

Behavior is ____ or is not ___ characteristic of me.

4. **Impatience ith the rate things occur.** Type A's feel a constant sense of urgency, thus they are impatient with the rate at which things occur. They lack tolerance for time-delayed tasks; that is, they become irritated if they have to wait on others before they can begin their work. They can't stand "pokey" drivers on the highway, and get extremely agitated when waiting in line.

Behavior is ____ or is not ___ characteristic of me.

5. **Preoccupied hen others are talking.** Type A's may not be good listeners. They are so bullied by the work load they've taken on that they grow impatient when others are slowly developing their thoughts. Consequently, they may dominate the conversation in order to determine the topics. They may be preoccupied with their own plans when others are talking. They may wait for others to pause for breath and then jump in to finish their sentence for them because they can say it faster.

Behavior is ____ or is not ___ characteristic of me.

6. **Vague guilty feelings hen not busy at "producing."** Because Type A's believe that their worth is derived solely from their productions, they are nervous and self-critical when not working. They may go on vacation and take more

work with them than they leave at home. If their spouses lecture them about the need to drop work issues and to join in family activities, they may dutifully do so while all the time resenting it. On a vacation, Type A's secretly wish to be home where work can be done. Instead of appreciating a respite from the tyranny of their work schedules, they feel uneasy and perhaps guilty for the "nonproductive" time spent.

Behavior is _____ or is not ___ characteristic of me.

7. **No compassion for other Type A s.** Type A's may not get along particularly well unless they are sharing the same project. Each will feel justified in conscripting available resources for his or her unfinished projects. They will often feel, but not necessarily consciously recognize, threatened by other Type A's and find themselves frequently in competition with others.

Behavior is _____ or is not ___ characteristic of me.

8. **Taking little time to develop oneself mentally and spiritually.** Type A's are addicted to doing things. Consequently, they infrequently take time out to clarify their values and to prioritize their activities. Their lives are cluttered with tasks—important ones and not so important ones, and they often don't draw clear distinctions between them. If there is something to be done, they can't rest fully until it has been accomplished. Consequently, they may neglect the development of themselves mentally and spiritually. They may not allow themselves the *luxury* of reading just for self-development. In the worst case scenario, they may feel spiritually bankrupt.

Behavior is_____ or is not ___ characteristic of me.

9. **Characteristic nervous gestures.** The tension associated with the drivenness of the Type A behavior pattern sometimes leads to telltale symptoms, such as facial tics (where the muscles in the face twitch involuntarily), clenched fists and jaws, and the grinding of the teeth. Twenty million Americans engage in *bruxism*—the grinding of the teeth both during the day and at night. If the practice is not stopped, the person may cycle into TMJ—temporal mandibular joint disorder. TMJ causes excruciating pain, as the temporal and mandibular bones put pressure on the trigeminal nerve attaching to facial muscles.

Behavior is_____ or is not ___ characteristic of me.

Now, add your scores across the nine Type A behaviors. Although there is no formal scoring key for this list, you might consider yourself to be Type A if you can honestly claim five or more of these behaviors. Don't despair if you feel the shoe fits; we have good news for you! First, it's not all your fault—as we will discuss next, our culture fosters many Type A tendencies. Second, we will discuss recent research that suggests that Type A personality traits are harmful only when accompanied by certain other personal characteristics. And third, we will offer suggestions for changing the Type A behaviors that you find most problematic.

The Culture Breeds Type A Characteristics

If you believe you are Type A, you are not alone. Friedman and Rosenman estimate that 60 percent of Americans have Type A patterns. The socialization process seems to encourage Type A attitudes. Expressions such as "Time is money," "Idleness is the Devil's workshop," and "A stitch in time saves nine" were a part of American folklore from the earliest days of the Republic. Many such aphorisms were included in the old McGuffrey readers that were part of the school curriculum used widely through the early part of the nineteenth century. The values implicit in such aphorisms seem to be deeply etched in the American character. In his extensive studies of achievement, the Harvard professor David McClelland (1985) found Americans to score higher on achievement motivation than citizens of any other country. This need for achievement is compatible with the fact that Americans work longer hours than workers in other developed nations.

McClelland and his colleague, Jemmott (1980), discovered a correlation between highly promotable managers and Type A characteristics. These managers had a high need for power, a low need for affiliation, and a high need for self-control (inhibition). They were apt to say, "I don't get ulcers. I give them!" Actually, however, much stress results from the throttling of your feelings, and sure enough, these managers were more frequently ill than were managers with lesser power needs but greater needs for affiliation.

Charismatic Type A's

Recent research suggests that the original picture of the coronary-prone individual needs qualification. It now appears that the Type A behavior pattern alone may not predispose the person to coronary artery disease. For instance, there is some evidence that Type A individuals with charismatic qualities may actually be healthier than mellower Type B's. Even though these charismatic types are just as speedy, driven, and ambitious as other Type A's, they are more emotionally expressive and less hostile—probably because they are more effective in enlisting the help of others in accomplishing their goals. Because of their charisma, they draw others to themselves and are successful as leaders. They laugh infectiously, move a lot, and appear to be genuinely confident. As a result they are less prone to heart disease.

The Lethal Trio

It now seems likely that only part of the Type A pattern may predispose the person to coronary artery disease. Later researchers who reviewed the original data on which the Type A behavior pattern was based were able to pinpoint the toxic elements in the syndrome. According to Redford Williams and his colleagues (1980) at Duke University, the toxic part appears to be hostility associated with cynical contempt. Hostility is an enduring trait where anger is directed toward people. Anger itself is situational and can be directed toward anything. Males have higher scores on measures of hostility than females and are at greater risk of coronary artery disease (Engebretson and Matthews 1992; Manuck and Saab 1992). Hostile, cynical Type A's are deeply suspicious and constantly on guard against others whom they believe are dishonest, antisocial, and/or immoral. Hostile people have frequent attacks of anger that put them in a near constant state of stress.

This constant stress arousal increases the production of epinephrine and norepinephrine. These in turn sharply elevate the heart beat and blood pressure, they increase levels of "bad" cholesterol (LDL) and decrease levels of "good" cholesterol (HDL), all risk factors for heart disease.

Dembroski, MacDougall, Williams, Haney, and Blumental (1985) round out our understanding of predisposing personality factors with their conclusion that hostility is most damaging when accompanied by the tendency to swallow your anger. In short, the research seems to point to a fatal trio of predisposing factors: the Type A behavior pattern *interacting with* a cynical distrust of others and strangled hostility. This lethal combination is depicted in Figure 7-5. Note that the lethal combination increases your risk of infectious diseases and cancer (through the suppression of your immune system) as well.

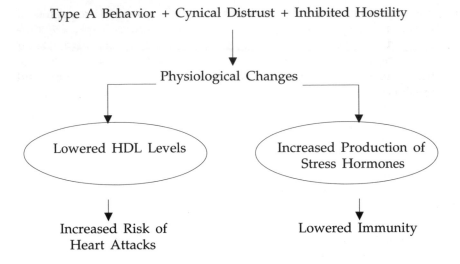

Figure 7-5. Lethal elements of the coronary-prone personality.

Treating the Type A Personality

Type A behavior may be encouraged by factors such as parental expectations for achievement coupled with frequent criticism and an intensely competitive atmosphere (Girdano, Everly, and Dusek 1997). Although there may be some genetic contributors to the syndrome, Type A behavior is mostly learned, and well-designed treatment programs are likely to modify the pattern in healthful ways. In the 1980s, Myer Friedman and his colleagues in the Western Collaborative Group Study in San Francisco created a treatment program for Type A's. They found that Type A's who had suffered a heart attack and subsequently received instruction in changing their Type A behavior (including techniques for reducing anger) experienced significantly fewer incidents of second heart attacks and deaths than a comparable group who received only routine cardiac rehabilitation.

We suggest steps here that can be taken to treat the symptoms of Type A personality, but we caution those of you who are Type A that often more wide-ranging, wellness-enhancing practices are necessary to get at the heart of Type A syndrome. Some of these broader steps will be discussed in chapters 8 and 10.

Relief from "Hurry Sickness."

If chronic hostility, swallowed or expressed, contributes to coronary artery disease, the remedy of course would be to avoid hostility. Much of the hostility experienced by Type A's is a result of hurry sickness—the attempt to do more in less time. Type A's operate under unrealistic time constraints imposed by *themselves*. Their over-ambitiousness cause them to attempt multiple tasks at the same time, creating frustration that leads to irritation, resentment, and hostility.

The antidote for hurry sickness is to remind yourself in as many ways as possible that *life is a journey, not a destination!* Imagine how ridiculous it would be for a pianist to attempt to finish a beautiful concerto as quickly as possible. Or consider trying to consume all of the food you will eat over the course of a lifetime in one sitting. Yet some of us act as though the goal of life is to finish. This hurrying approach is worse yet if we add the perfectionist's touch—now the goal becomes not only to hurry up and finish things but to get them *right* as well! Such attitudes add unnecessary grimness to life.

Lao Tsu, the founder of Taoism, writes of the "ten thousand things" that make up life. Type A's are so busy trying to finish the ten thousand things that they lose their sense of what is important. They are tyrannized by the trivia. If Type A's are to experience any sense of self-possession, they must challenge the mindless busyness that threatens to consume them. They must understand that nothing is so inefficient as doing something that doesn't need being done in the first place. They need to heed the admonition of Barry Stevens (1985) in his book titled *Don't Push the River*.

Impatience: A Symptom.

The impatience that Type A's characteristically experience is often the result of underestimating the time it takes to complete a task. Working under unrealisitic, self-imposed time limits, they become angered by their "slowness" instead of adjusting their expectations. If this sounds familiar you may want to develop more respect for the complexity of tasks and more tolerance for unexpected hurdles that arise. One helpful technique is to add a 30 percent factor to your estimate of the time needed to complete a task.

"No": The Magic Word.

Impatience is often a sign that you are not invested in an activity. Because they are addicted to getting things done, Type A's may exercise little choice over what they do. Consequently, they often find themselves frantically working at things that are of little consequence to them. The antidote for this impatience is to make more conscious choices of tasks, to save time and energy for tasks that really matter. Learning to say "no" will be of great help in clearing out tasks that are not personally rewarding.

Pace Your Efforts.

Pace your efforts so you do not work in spasms. Paul Simon said it nicely in "The 59th Street Bridge Song." "Slow down, you move too fast. You've got to make the morning last." The goal is not to shirk your duties but rather to do them with some degree of centeredness, to remain reasonably calm and collected while focusing on one task at a time.

Renegotiate Deadlines.

People suffering from hurry sickness are reluctant to ask that deadlines be extended. They view such requests as evidence of their incompetence, disorganization, or sloth. Consequently, they place their bodies under great strain in a frantic effort to finish on time. Renegotiating deadlines, however, is often expected and acceptable to others.

Clarify Your Values.

Humans are doers and problem-solvers. The mind can be thought of as a problem-solving biocomputer. If the mind is not presented with problems from the outside, it creates them from within so it can practice solving them. Without disciplining ourselves, we constantly worry about things—big things, little things, it doesn't matter. Worry fills the mind like gas fills a container. Just as gas molecules spread out to fill the space, worries, whether big or little, fill the space in our minds. Many of us are Type A in the sense that we are constantly worrying and constantly doing.

When overwhelmed by a spate of tasks, inspect each and ask yourself, "In what way is this task contributing to the welfare of myself or others?" If you cannot give yourself a satisfactory answer, drop the task from your list. Stop doing things merely because they are there.

Set aside time daily to sort out your personal values. What is it that you want to do with your life? One way of answering this question is to try to imagine yourself lying on a hospital bed reviewing your life just hours before death. How would you have to live your life *now* to feel a sense of integrity in that hour? Clearly identify a few things that would be of importance to you in that moment, and start doing them *now*! Blow away the chaff and make more room in your life for the truly important things.

Once you know what is important to you, spend as much time as possible on activities that support these values. If your work seems to have integrity, to have meaning for you, it will be easier for you to commit yourself to it. Suzanne Kobasa (1979) found that commitment to work was one of the most effective buffers against stress-induced illness. Work that fits your values will provide you with rich psychological rewards. In searching for such work heed the words of the mystic Don Juan in Carlos Castenada's A *Separate Reality* (1972), when he advised his young Bolivian apprentice:

> Look at every path closely and deliberately. Try it as many times as you think necessary. . . . [Ask yourself], "Does this path have a heart?" If it does, the path is good; if it doesn't, it is of no use. [A path with a heart] makes for a joyful journey. . . . [But following a path without a heart] will make you curse your life.

Form More Trusting Attitudes.

Although prior experiences may have led you to form negative views of others, be aware that such views often become self-fulfilling prophecies. To some extent we are responsible for creating our own social environments. When you believe others are unfriendly or exploitative, your approach to them can create defensiveness in them. Subsequently, you conclude that you were right—they *are* unfriendly, exploitative, or otherwise unpleasant. If others have injured you in the past, it may take a lot of hard work over considerable time to learn to trust. But without the hard work, you are likely to be frequently stressed by your contacts with others. Try running experiments. When you are tempted to approach others defensively, force yourself to become more self-disclosing, take greater risks with others, and see what happens. If your friendly overtures are met with reciprocal warmth, your jaundiced views of others will begin to give way to a more trusting set of views. Remember, cynical distrust is a part of the "fatal trio" that predisposes you to heart attacks and infectious diseases.

As we have seen, ample evidence suggests that personality traits can contribute greatly to both stress and overall health. Whether you feel you exhibit characteristics of a thrill-seeking personality, an anxious-reactive personality, a carcinogenic personality, or a coronary-prone personality, the first step in lowering stress is often to recognize how your personality may be compounding your problems with stress. Once you've identified these personality factors, you can set out to cope with these tendencies more healthfully.

Chapter 8

Overcoming Stressful Patterns of Thinking

> *Projection makes perception. The world you see is what you gave it, nothing more than that. It is the witness to your state of mind, the outside picture of an inward condition. As a man thinketh, so does he perceive. Therefore, seek not to change the world, but choose to change your mind about the world.*
>
> —Anonymous

Although the stress response is made up of physical reactions, it is the power of thought that triggers the response into action. It is the meaning that we assign to events that determines whether we will respond stressfully or calmly. Over the course of a single day we contact many people and experience countless events. With split-second alacrity we make judgments about them and respond accordingly. We judge whether such experiences hold significance for us, whether they constitute threats, irrelevancies, or potential rewards. We are not always correct in our judgments. We sometimes are later relieved to find that the "boogeyman" we saw was actually harmless. And sometimes we are disappointed to find that the promising engagement proves to be a dud. In chapter 6 we emphasized the importance of preventing stress by increasing our general resistance to it. In this chapter we again are concerned with prevention—preventing stress by eliminating conditioned patterns of negative thinking that cause us to be hypersensitive to situations and events.

Perceptual Filters

Quite early in life you develop patterns in the ways you view others, the world, and yourself. We refer to these patterns as *perceptual filters*. You look out at the world through these filters, and they largely determine what you see. Parents, caretakers, or other agents of society influence these perceptual filters. Some were constructed from our own unique experiences. For example, some people learn very early in life to trust and respect authority figures, while others do not. Individuals carrying the "don't trust authority" filter likely will be disinclined to accept direction or guidance from those in positions of responsibility. When these views correspond faithfully to reality, they offer good cognitive maps by which to live. Being suspicious of authorities who don't have your best interests in mind, for instance, can be a good thing. If these views are irrational, however they may create a great deal of distress. Even a benevolent boss at work will tire quickly of employees who constantly question instructions, and will likely decide to find others who will!

Most perceptual filters lead you to make accurate interpretations of your experiences. However, some cause you to view your experiences inappropriately which causes you a great deal of stress. You filter your perceptions of the world through your needs or desires. Your needs can bully you, dominate your consciousness, and tyrannically drive your behavior. Realizing this form of tyranny, the ancient sage said, "If you would make a man happy, add not to his riches but take away from his desires." In a 1987 poll conducted by the *Chicago Tribune*, people earning less than $30,000 a year indicated that $50,000 would fulfill their dreams. In the same survey people making over $100,000 a year said they would need to make $250,000 to be happy (*Chicago Tribune* 1987). Research has consistently shown that the goal posts keep being extended as the income goes up. In terms of motivation, it's not the amount of the reward but the difference between the reward and your baseline income that brings satisfaction (Parducci 1995). Strong needs result in selective perception. If you are hungry, you scan the landscape for food. If you are frightened, you focus on those features of the environment that constitute potential threats. If you are sexually deprived, you may scan for possible sexual partners.

Because most needs are met in a social environment, the ability to negotiate successfully for the meeting of those needs becomes critical to happiness. People who lack such negotiation skills may go for extended periods without their needs being met. Basic needs that are chronically unmet can dominate your perceptions. Eventually these unmet needs form the perceptual filters that limit what you see in life. Consequently, your views of what is correspond less accurately with reality, and, thus, your information base becomes a poor guide for behavior. Once these filters are frozen in place, emotional reactions to events and persons become locked into place as well. The development of such inaccurate perceptual filters is the basis for self-defeating, neurotic lifestyles. And just as the ophthalmologist performs cataract surgery to remove the cloudy lens of the eyes, we need to replace self-defeating perceptual filters with ones that more accurately represent reality.

Landscapers and Networkers: Filters in Action

We all have known people who seem to view everybody and everything through dark perceptual filters that create a jaundiced view of the world. While attending graduate school, Ken worked for a landscaper who held such a disgruntled view of the world. He complained endlessly about demanding customers; irresponsible help; the costs of plants, shrubs, and sod; and uncooperative weather that threatened the growth of his plants. His half-paranoid views of customers, workers, and acquaintances created interminable conflicts with others. His mood was somber, his health in jeopardy, and his financial condition shaky. Ken attempted to avoid him as much as possible, but his boss seemed to like him and frequently sought his company.

One day he spotted Ken as he was leaving city hall. He came running up waving a slip of paper and yelling loudly, "This proves it! This proves the Kansas City police force is corrupt!" Ken thought perhaps he had uncovered a scandal that would soon appear across the headlines of the *Kansas City Star*. But his boss merely told him that the police had given him a traffic ticket. Ken was supposed to believe that some great injustice had been done him. He was telling the wrong person, however, as Ken knew him to be one of the rudest, most aggressive drivers he had ever seen. He drove with one hand on the steering wheel and one on his horn, and he figuratively drove over others as though he were in a Sherman tank.

When he finished criticizing the police department, he began a long litany of complaints about other public officials. When he had verbally massacred them as well, he began complaining about his wife. He complained of her cooking, her housekeeping, and her looks. You probably get the picture, because you've probably known people with equally negative attitudes.

Perhaps the most important lesson here is that such individuals create their own realities through their selective filtering of experiences. No law requires you to automatically assume the worst of other people! Surely some deserve this distinction, but much of the time the social landscape is wide open. Just like you, other people are scanning their environment in attempting to separate opportunities from threats. If you are prone to see others as unfriendly and unhelpful, you may be reluctant to ask for help when it would be readily forthcoming.

An interesting example of this concerns one of the most essential aspects of job hunting: networking. For many jobs, especially those in the professional ranks, one of the most effective job search strategies involves using personal and professional contacts to locate desirable jobs. Because many of the best jobs are obtained this way, those who rely on classified ads or public postings of openings can lose out. However, the vast majority of individuals are shut out of this hidden job market because they are uncomfortable about imposing on others for information about possible openings. This filter (Other people don't want to be bothered with my job hunting woes) can be both inaccurate and limiting. The vast majority of people who are in a position to help others find employment are happy to do so. Employers are often extremely grateful to employees who help them find other competent employees. In addition, those who are successful and enjoy their work often find it gratifying to help others gain similar positions. The point is that it can be vital to your happiness to look constantly for ways to revise your perceptual filters in more adaptive ways.

The idea that behavior can be changed by thought control is hardly new. It has been stated time and again in the worlds great literature. Hamlet says, "There is nothing either good or bad, but thinking makes it so." In the Old Testament we read, "As a man thinketh in his heart, so is he." In the New Testament, "Finally, brethren, whatsoever things are true . . . honest . . . just . . . pure . . . lovely . . . of good report; if there be any virtue, and if there be any praise, think on these things." Right thinking is one of the chief practices recommended by Buddhists for the good life. Faith in the importance of thinking as a guide to behavior underlies the practice of advertising, political brainwashing, and more legitimate forms of education.

Placebos and Nocebos

The power of beliefs to influence behavior is clearly demonstrated in the effect of placebos and nocebos. When early physicians were frustrated by their lack of effective medicines they often would fall back on placebos. *Placebo* is a Latin word that means "I shall be pleasant." In other words a placebo is some substance or experience that instills the belief that things will get better. The ancient Egyptians prescribed crocodile dung, the hoof of an ass, and flyspecks that worked as placebos, and later physicians prescribed the spermatic fluid of frogs, the flesh of vipers, and powdered mummies. Yuck! Three-fourths of the time pain relief from placebos is as effective as an injection of morphine. Two placebo pills are more effective than one; and a placebo is more effective if given intravenously (Justice 1988)

Any intervention that enhances positive expectations and a sense of control can initiate the placebo response, and no deceit is necessary, according to Blair Justice (1988), a medical researcher at the University of Texas Medical Center in Houston. In one study patients were told that they would be given sugar pills and that these pills had helped a number of people and might also help them as well. All but one of the patients showed improvement in a week. In a more recent study it appeared that blood pressure might be controlled in some hypertensive patients simply by telling them that the act of regular monitoring produces a lowering effect and then asking them to check their pressure at frequent intervals. Believing they had an enhanced sense of control over their hypertension resulted in a positive placebo effect. Michael Gazzaniga (1988), however, points out that the analgesic effect from placebos tends to be short-lived, and the placebo effect works for somatic pain only, as opposed to internal, visceral pain.

In his book *The Healing Heart*, Norman Cousins (1983) tells of a remarkable recovery as a result of the placebo effect. The patient was critically ill with an irreparably compromised cardiac muscle for which all therapeutic means had been exhausted. During rounds, his physician, Dr. Lown, mentioned to his resident interns that the patient had a "wholesome gallop," actually a sign of significant pathology, and usually indicative of a failing heart. Several months later the patient came for the checkup in a remarkable state of recovery. He told Dr. Lown that he knew what had made him better and exactly when it had occurred. He said, "Thursday morning when you entered with your troops, something happened that changed everything. You listened to my heart; you seemed pleased by the findings and announced to those standing about my bed that I had a wholesome gallop." The patient reasoned that he must have had a lot of kick to his heart and therefore could not possibly be dying.

Although placebos often improve health, nocebos may impair our health. A nocebo is a substance or event that convinces you that you will get worse. A radiologist noticed an internist friend coughing and suggested that he have a lung X-ray. A spot was found that suggested metastasized lung cancer. The internist died within three months of hearing the bad news. However, going through X-ray files later the radiologist found another X-ray of the same internist two years earlier, with the same spot on his lung.

W. B. Joy concluded from his medical practice that "Healing does not rest in the hands of a selected few, but in the hands of every human being . . . no matter what physicians do, they can only augment the healing process of the body itself" (1969, p. 129). And R. S. Elliott (1986) wrote, "Whatever gives us an increased sense of control—whether its love, faith, or cognitive coping—seems to mobilize our self-healing process. Because thinking has the power of life and death, we should cultivate our thoughts as carefully as we cultivate our gardens."

Private Reality

You create the worlds you occupy by your perceptions. The world for some people is a cornucopia of rewards and pleasantries. For others it is a highly stressful, exhausting stage upon which they act out their unhappy scripts. Some people create infernos of the mind, a virtual hell on earth. The constant replaying of stressful scenarios such as personal vendettas bent on revenge or fears of failure creates lives full of stress and self-inflicted punishment. When people are locked in to such mind-sets, their energies are monopolized, their moods somber, and their ties to others weaker. Such states cause them to live inside their heads, limiting their contact with the outside world.

Many people adopt negative addictions to escape the mental infernos they have created for themselves. They exchange their active misery for a passive, zombie-like existence. Others, however, have learned to alter their mental states in an exquisitely appropriate manner. They share basic consciousness with us most of the time, but they have learned ways to escape the squirrel cage at will for purposes of centering, restoration, and creation.

Virtually all forms of psychotherapy attempt to help clients change their views about self and others. In this way all are concerned with impacting the consciousness of clients. Psychotherapists seek to help clients to "wake up," to substitute consciousness for unconsciousness, awareness for unawareness, mindfulness for mindlessness. Freud's early dictum to therapists and clients was, "The unconscious shall be made conscious." So the goal of most therapies is to help the tortured client conjure up self-limiting beliefs about self, others, and the world and to replace them with more functional ones. Clients learn to re-frame their experiences, to trade in their negative perceptual filters for more positive ones, to use more uplifting labels for their experiences.

The work of re-birthing your mental life is indeed challenging. The first task is to identify the cloudy perceptual filters that dim the sunlight in your life. Then, onto the daily work of replacing the cloudy filters with transparent ones that allow for a more objective view of things.

Like psychotherapy, religious practice has always been concerned with enlightening devotees, changing their views, and teaching them new labels for their experience. This concern is evident in some of the earliest religious writings. In the Judeo-Christian story of creation, Jahweh places man in the garden and parades the newly created earthly creatures before him to be given names. Since labels powerfully affect behavior, the act of naming is itself an act of creation. In one sense, Adam created the world by labeling his observations.

In one sense this creation-by-labeling is the message of quantum physics, post-modernism, feminist psychology, and multiculturalism, and other modes of modern thought. The quantum theorists, for instance, maintain that we determine reality by the way we set up our investigation. If the experiment is set up in one way, light appears to consist of particles. If it is set up differently, light appears to consist of waves. The actual nature of light, then, appears to elude us, for under certain conditions both views seem nicely supported. In one sense, the observer seems to create the reality by the vantage point she assumes. The reality becomes different depending upon the perspective she holds. One is reminded of the Sufi tale regarding the three blind men who each described the elephant from his own vantage point. Each concentrated on a separate part of the elephant and, consequently, offered descriptions of the elephant that were radically different. For such reasons, Edwin Schroeder, the German quantum physicist, maintained that "Reality is a convenient fiction."

Similarly, constructionist and narrative positions in psychology maintain that we individually create our private worlds by labeling our experiences of persons and events according to our individual perspectives. Once these mental templates become hardened into lasting guides to behavior, we become imprisoned behind bars of our own fashioning. Some of the mental spaces we inhabit are lovely, while others sentence us to spend our days in quiet desperation. Some spaces offer exciting vistas, while others cramp the human spirit.

Breaking Negative Thought Patterns

What most people don't understand is that negative thoughts actually change brain chemistry, and continuing such thoughts over time rewires the circuitry of the brain. To think is to *practice brain chemistry*. Thoughts consist of mental activity that is mediated by the effects of brain chemicals called neuropeptides. Change your thoughts and you change the neuropeptides that dictate what you feel and how you behave. Change your thought patterns long enough, and you actually change the circuitry of the brain.

The control of your thoughts becomes a powerful therapy for eliminating stressful emotional reactions. There are five levels at which you can attempt to influence stressful thought patterns. These levels are depicted in Figure 8-1. Level I approaches seek to desensitize you to specific stressors. Level II approaches attempt to suppress stressful self-talk. Level III approaches aim to replace irrational self-

Level I
Change Conditioned Reactions
　↘
　Level II
　Suppress Stressful Self-Talk
　　↘
　　Level III
　　Replace Irrational Beliefs
　　　↘
　　　Level IV
　　　Correct Distorted Perceptual Processes
　　　　↘
　　　　Level V
　　　　Alter Basic Consciousness

Figure 8-1. Levels of attack on stressful thinking.

talk and beliefs with more functional ones. Level IV approaches are designed to correct distorted perceptual processes. And Level V approaches are designed to change basic consciousness itself. The rest of this chapter is devoted to a discussion of the first four of these approaches. Level V approaches for creating a serene, stress-free consciousness is the topic of chapter 9.

Level I: Desensitizing Specific Stressors

Much of the time the stress response is triggered by conscious thinking. At times, however, it is automatically triggered by conditioned stimuli such as phobic objects or events. Fear of heights, fear of closed or open spaces, fear of authority figures, fear of flying, fear of examinations, and fear of public speaking may all reach phobic levels. When associations have been established between nonhurtful events and experiences that cause fear, we say the person has been sensitized to the event. Actually, the brain is hardwired to sensitize us to sources of danger in our environment. But it appears that nature's intent in designing the brain was so focused on this function that it didn't consider the possibility of overkill.

Evidence for the Power of Conditioning

An understanding of how conditioning can affect immune functioning gave driving force to psychoimmunology, the science of the effect of psychological states on the immune system. The doubts of physicians regarding such effects gave way in the face of experiments conducted by Robert Ader, a psychologist at the University of Rochester School of Medicine and Dentistry, and Nicholas Cohen, an immunologist. They administered cyclophosphamide, a drug that suppresses the immune system, in a saccharine solution to rats. The drug, as expected, depressed immune functioning. The combination of the saccharine and cyclophosphamide was administered repeatedly with the same results. Apparently in the minds of the rats the strong taste of the saccharine was associated with the cyclophosphamide, because later administrations of the saccharine solution without the cyclophosphamide resulted in immunosuppression as well.

Herbert Spector, of the National Institutes of Health, conducted a similar study. He administered cyclophosphamide to rats that were simultaneously exposed to the strong scent of camphor. As with the experiment by Ader and Cohen, the rats eventually experienced suppression of the immune system from the scent of the camphor alone. A second group of rats were given poly IC, a drug that strengthens immune functioning, simultaneously with exposure to the scent of camphor, and later they would experience a fortification of the immune system from the same scent. So the scent of camphor would in one case cause immunosuppression and in another a strengthening of immune functioning.

Association Is the Key

The mechanism used by nature to sensitize us to potential threats is association. In the fourth century B.C., the Greek philosopher Aristotle noted that two ideas tend to be remembered together if associated in time. Early in the twentieth century, Ivan Petrovich Pavlov (1928) demonstrated the power of association to condition emotional effects. In a series of classic experiments he conditioned hungry dogs to salivate to the ringing of a bell merely by pairing the bell with the presentation of food paste. The repeated associations invested the sound of the bell with the ability to elicit salivation from the dog. In short, in the dogs' minds the sound of the bell ringing was a signal that the trainer would soon give it food paste. The reflexive salivation was an anticipatory response. The bell now had "signal value."

Recent investigations of such classic conditioning reveal that signal value is conferred on whatever has drawn the learner's attention at the time of the association. Because the person sometimes is attending to irrelevant stimuli while undergoing stressful experiences, irrelevant stimuli sometimes are bonded to the stressful experiences and take on the ability to trigger the stressful reaction. You can imagine how chance associations can set up such superstitious beliefs as those that suggest that walking under a ladder or having a black cat cross in front of you will bring bad luck. Irrational fears caused by chance associations are referred to as phobic reactions.

Not all superstitious reactions are stressful. Athletes are particularly likely to engage in superstitious behaviors. For example, NBA great Pete Maravich insisted on wearing the same socks throughout his NBA career. It seems that he had noticed that he was wearing the socks while having a sensational game. He superstitiously attributed his successful performance to the socks and felt insecure when playing without them. Joe Theismann, who led the Washington Redskins football team to a Super Bowl title at the end of the 1982 season, had an elaborate series of rituals he performed before every game. He walked from one end of the football field to the other and read the latest *People* magazine from cover to cover.

Interestingly, one anthropologist who studied superstitious rituals among baseball players found that infield players tended to engage in such behaviors more often than those in the outfield. Infielders, who are forced to rely on instinct and reflexes to play their position, are apparently more likely to rely on superstitious beliefs than outfielders who, because they have more time to react to events on the field, feel more in control of events.

Based on the power of associations, one can guess how the cartoon character Linus became addicted to his security blanket. Most of our emotional reactions—joyful or stressful—are established through the bonding of associated events. Cluttering up your life with unnecessary fearful reactions creates a highly stressful lifestyle.

The intensity of negative signals, however, steadily diminishes with time. Thus, the influence of weaker positive thought signals on emotional arousal becomes relatively greater as the initial shock to the nervous system from conditioned stimuli wears off. Accordingly, there is much value in positive thinking, for it can greatly shorten the time involved in recovering from conditioned arousal.

This hopeful picture is based on the assumption that when suffering painful emotional arousal you will respond with positive thoughts. Unfortunately, most people actually heighten their arousal further with *negative* thinking. They often exaggerate the seriousness of the demand and underestimate their resources for dealing with it. Because stress is a result of perceiving that your resources are inadequate for the demands being confronted, such thinking strengthens the effects of conditioned signals and maintains painful arousal longer.

Deconditioning Procedures

When conditioned emotional responses become too costly, a kind of radical surgery is necessary to decondition them. The most common form of deconditioning in psychotherapeutic settings is systematic desensitization, a procedure in which images of the feared experience are associated with feelings of deep relaxation. When images of the feared stimulus become associated with relaxation, they lose their ability to initiate the fearful response. The procedure is quite effective and can take as little as ten to twenty sessions.

Self-initiated desensitization is possible, but it's more difficult than desensitization with a psychotherapist's aid. If you attempt to desensitize yourself to stress-inducing events, you must understand that exposure to the event is an absolutely essential part of the plan. If your fear is not totally incapacitating, begin with gradual exposure to the real event or situation. If the fear is so intense that such exposure is out of the question, choose exposures to imagined aspects of the event. It is critical that either real or imagined exposure to the event be gradual. The event or situation must be first broken down into steps representing parts of the event. These parts are then arranged in order of the magnitude of the fear elicited. For example, if your fear is riding the subway, you should identify the behaviors necessary for doing so such as approaching the ticket counter, purchasing the ticket, going through the turnstile, boarding the train, awaiting the call for your station, and leaving the subway station. List the steps in order from least to most anxiety-provoking. If you are using imaginary exposure, you first become deeply relaxed, perhaps using one of the relaxation procedures discussed earlier, and then you visualize the lowest step on your hierarchy. Repeat the visualization until you have developed tolerance for this early step, and then move on to the next step. Continue this process until you have become desensitized to each behavior involved in the fearful event.

If your fear is not overwhelming, it is much quicker to expose yourself to the real event, provided you are able to approach the event in a relatively calm manner. It may be necessary to experience the event only partially at first. In the illustration above, this might mean merely approaching the ticket counter repeatedly until the fear comes under control. Often you will be more successful if you are in the company of a reassuring person who is aware of your fear. Remember that whether you are dealing with imaginary scenes or real situations, there is no lasting progress without exposure. In some form or another you must gain the courage to expose yourself to the fearful situation.

If conditioned fears relate to events that seldom happen to you, you may choose to live with the stress rather than devote considerable time (and perhaps money) to a desensitization program. However, if you frequently experience the event, or if it interferes significantly with your life, it may be wise to seek professional treatment or to attempt to desensitize yourself.

Level II: Thought Suppression

There are times when stressful thoughts can so monopolize your mental energy that it is difficult to fulfill your ordinary duties. Usually it is best to recognize the troublesome situation and attempt to deal with it. There are two circumstances within which it is best to suppress the troubling thoughts. First, at times you may be helpless to reduce or eliminate the stressor. Second, sometimes other issues can be so critical that it is best to delay efforts to deal with the stressor.

It is important to understand that we are recommending suppression and not repression. Repression is a concept first introduced by Sigmund Freud's school of psychoanalysis that refers to thoughts or impulses that have gone underground; that is, they have been restrained from conscious awareness because they may conflict with your moral values. Repressed content is unfinished business that requires a great deal of mental energy to keep hidden from consciousness. It is unhealthy, for the repressed impulse may continue to gain strength over time, requiring more and more psychic energy to keep it in check. At some point it may explode into inappropriate behaviors or may be converted into physical symptoms. In contrast, suppression is a conscious effort to turn your attention away from the troublesome thought in the interest of dealing with more immediate issues, and it may be the wisest behavior at a given moment.

We'll give you a personal example. Ken recently underwent laser surgery to correct astigmatism and farsightness. He had chosen to do so on the strength of multiple testimonies of patients who were happy with the results. Perhaps because of Ken's age, the surgery required multiple "enhancements," that is, additional surgeries to improve the results over a four-month period. To this point the procedure has not worked well. While Ken is able to read (with some difficulty), his far vision is quite blurry.

Because vision is so very important to Ken's activities, the temporary handicap is a constant source of irritation for him. Because he is convinced that the ophthalmologist is competent and that he is doing his best, there seems nothing reasonable for Ken to do presently other than to tolerate the inconvenience. His attention is constantly drawn to the problem. Consequently, he engages in a great deal of thought suppression to save mental energy, to reign in irritation, and to get on with his duties. His program for suppressing thoughts about the poor vision largely consists of two behaviors: self-talk and diverting his attention.

When the troublesome thought appears, he tell himself that he is taking reasonable steps to improve the vision, such as taking proper medication, consulting with the physician, and undergoing the recommended surgical enhancements. A healthy part of him will not allow him peace until he has committed himself to an appropriate course of action to deal with the problem. As we discussed in chapter 5 suppressing thoughts about a stressor that needs to be dealt with is neither wise nor effective.

Ken also attempts to divert his attention from the stressful thoughts. Cognitive-behavior therapists, those who use psychotherapy primarily to effect changes in thinking, have used "thought-stopping" with clients who experience obsessive thought patterns.

Stressful thinking often has a snowball effect. An insignificant problem may become overwhelming if it is endlessly processed. Once on a roll, the thoughts seem to have a life of their own and are difficult to stop. Thought-stopping is most effective when it is initiated early in the buildup of the obsessive thinking. The training comes in four stages. First the therapist yells, "Stop!" while the client is audibly reciting the obsessive thought. Next, the therapist again yells, "Stop" while the client is merely thinking the thought. Then the client is instructed to loudly pound the table (or snap a rubber band attached to his or her wrist) while saying the thought aloud, and lastly to do so while merely thinking the thought. Unfortunately, few empirical studies have evaluated the procedure, and the results are believed to be somewhat questionable. The technique's effectiveness is enhanced by conscious efforts to redirect your thinking to more pleasant experiences, such as visualizing a peaceful scene or seeking the company of a rewarding friend, for instance. Shifting the focus of attention to more neutral or more rewarding thoughts at the least will interrupt the cascading stressful thoughts.

The use of thought-stopping as a sort of emergency procedure for distracting yourself from troublesome thoughts may be useful in the short term. However, it can be extremely taxing to carry on over an extended period. Therefore, we will next focus on ways to eliminate stressful thinking in the long term.

Level III: Correcting Stressful Self-Talk and Beliefs

We are constantly talking to ourselves about the meaning of our experience. In a passage from Castaneda's (1972) *A Separate Reality*, Don Juan says, "The world is such-and-such or so-and-so only because we tell ourselves that is the way it is . . . You talk to yourself. You're not unique at that. Every one of us does that. We carry on internal talk . . . In fact, we maintain our world with our internal talk."

What you say to yourself largely reflects your beliefs about others and yourself. The relationship between self-talk and beliefs is reciprocal, that is, each influences the other. Both are integral parts of the mental content that dictates your behavior. Although it may appear that changing self-talk is a superficial way of attempting to change feelings and behavior, Deal and Williams (1988) found that immediate negative self-talk was more predictive of depression than measures of irrational beliefs.

Cognitive therapists attack both beliefs and self-talk. They know that over time, negative statements like "I'm not good enough to play in the orchestra" or "I always screw things up," damage your confidence because you begin to believe them. And when confidence in your ability dips, difficulties are more likely to be viewed stressfully. Therapists attempt to change such beliefs in two ways: First, they attempt to restructure the meaning the stressful event has for the client by offering information that challenges the client's self-defeating beliefs. In some cases this will mean challenging the motives that the client has attributed to the behavior of others. Your emotional reactions to the behavior of others depends considerably on your belief about why they behaved as they did. For example, if a street person waved his arms wildly and swore at you, your emotional reaction would depend on your interpretation of his motives. If you attributed his remarks to hatefulness, you likely would become quite angry. If you had been informed beforehand that he was mentally ill, however, you likely would feel awkward but not necessarily angry.

Cognitive therapists also encourage clients to run experiments based on their irrational beliefs. If, for instance, a young man believes that no girl would date him, he is asked to put the belief to a test. After receiving proper instruction regarding how to ask a girl for date, he is then given the task as a homework assignment. The choice of the girl he invites, of course, becomes important to the experiment. If the girl accepts the invitation, the self-defeating belief has been successfully challenged.

Behavior is strongly influenced by your views of the future. If you want to start a business, play the piano, or write a novel *and* you believe you are unlikely to succeed, you probably will never try. You are more likely to tell yourself, "I couldn't do that," and the self-statement would likely restrain you from trying. Self-expectations frequently make the difference between success and failure. Rosenthal (1966) maintained that self-expectations become self-fulfilling prophecies.

As we mentioned, these self-expectations are often revealed in self-talk. Another promising way of reducing stress is to replace nonfunctional self-talk with more functional self-talk. Research in the 1960s demonstrated the critical influence of self-talk on emotional reactions. Studies exposed participants to experiences designed to affect their self-talk. Afterwards, the researcher would measure the effect of these experiences on the performance of tasks that were sensitive to emotional mood. In one such study (Velton 1968), participants read statements constructed to create elation, depression, or a neutral mood state. True to the researcher's assumption, the group reading the elation statements out performed the other two groups on a series of emotionally sensitive tasks.

The words you use to refer to your experiences are powerful stimulants to emotions. Choose them carefully. Telling yourself that you are "hopping mad" or "scared to death" is likely to intensify your emotional reactions more than if you had used labels such as "irritated" or "excited." The important thing, of course, is that the words used to describe your experience are believable. If you wish to exercise more control over your emotional reactions, therefore, you should carefully monitor self-talk.

Check the Logic of Self-Talk

Most people seem to believe that their emotional reactions stem directly from what is happening to them. If they are angry, it is because the event is angering. If they are sad, it is because the situation is melancholic. If they are afraid, it is because the situation is scary. They often fail to understand that it is their interpretation of the event, and not the objective aspects of the event itself, that causes their reaction. You create anger, sadness, fear (or joy for that matter), by what you say to yourself about these events. Leo Tolstoy fully understood how self-talk influences behavior when he wrote of Russia's war effort in *War and Peace*, "We lost because we told ourselves we lost."

As we saw with the example of the cursing homeless man, a great deal of stress can come from assigning bad motives to others. Usually there are equally plausible explanations for behaviors. Say Sunday morning you don't receive your newspaper. That much is a fact. You will, of course, be disappointed, but beyond the understandable disappointment, your emotional reaction will be determined largely by your choice of an explanation for the event. If you say to yourself, "That kids irresponsible! He's probably slept in or had his mind somewhere else when he past my house," you could be right. On the other hand, perhaps he has become ill, or his bike had a flat, or the news courier failed to deliver his allotment. Any number of other reasons might account for his failure to deliver your paper. If you attributed the failure of delivery to any of these alternate explanations, your emotional reaction would be less stressful. If you actually don't know why you didn't receive your paper, it is best to entertain a more benign explanation for the sake of your emotions.

Once you realize that your emotional reactions follow directly from your beliefs and self-talk, you can no longer escape responsibility for them. You realize that it is your choice whether to become distressed by events or to take them in stride. You will feel a great deal more control when you realize that the key to your emotions resides in your head, not in the actions of others.

Beliefs That Create Stress

Albert Ellis (1973) argues that the tendency to choose disturbing explanations for events is a natural consequence of certain nonfunctional beliefs taught by society. He believes the following nonfunctional beliefs are widely prevalent in American culture:

Belief 1. I *should* be perfectly competent and masterful in my activities, and if I am not, I am a *worthless* person .

Belief 2. Others *should* treat me considerately and fairly, and if they don't, they are bad people.

Belief 3. The world *should* provide pleasure rather than pain for me, and life is horrible and unbearable if it doesn't.

These irrational, childish ideas influence our explanations for events. Because of them we construct faulty editorials that turn ordinary experiences into stressful ones. Ellis (1981) maintains that the elimination of these irrational ideas would make it difficult to become intensely emotionally distressed, or at least to sustain the distress for lengthy periods. Thus, you can greatly reduce the stress and misery in your life by exchanging these nonfunctional ideas for more reasonable ones.

Thoughts about the future affect your vulnerability to stress. Two thoughts are particularly likely to intensify your reactions to stressors: One is your belief about how long the stressor will last, and the other is your belief about whether things are getting better or worse. There is a natural tendency to believe that the stressful situation will last forever. Likewise it is difficult to recognize when things are getting better. The belief that the bad situation is temporary and that things are getting better are powerful allies for hope, and hope empowers us and lowers stressful arousal.

Level IV: Correcting Distorted Thinking

In addition to faulty beliefs and sabotaging self-talk, the manner in which you process information also may contribute to stress. Aaron Beck (1976) focuses on distorted cognitive processes that people use to process information about themselves and their environment. These cognitive processes become mental habits, and they strongly influence your construction of reality. The following thinking distortions are adapted from Beck's work.

Exaggerated Thinking

Many people have a tendency to exaggerate the seriousness of events out of proportion to reality. Such a tendency can lead them to conclude that they will never get anything right after making a single mistake. The exaggerated nature of the following statements is easily spotted. "John broke off our engagement. Now I know I'll never get married." "Susan is ten minutes late already. That tells me she didn't want to meet me in the first place." (Here the person also engages in mind reading.) "I made a C on that exam. There's no way under heaven that I'm gonna pass this class." "I *always* put things off when they are unpleasant." "People *never* have a good time with me." "Everything I do turns out wrong!" In such cases small bits of information are assigned enormous importance. In so doing you can make unjustifiable jumps in logic and draw conclusions from evidence that is either lacking or actually contrary to the conclusion reached. This logical error stems from creating general rules from single incidents.

All-or-Nothing Thinking

This is a kind of polarized thinking in which people think in extremes. In these cases only two possibilities are allowed: right or wrong, good or bad, always or never, all or nothing. They say things such as, "Either you're for me or against me." "Right is right, and wrong is wrong." Such dichotomous thinking obscures the many shades of opinion that are revealed by more discriminating thinking. You may conclude, "People always get bored with me." The global nature of this statement may cause you to be reluctant to be with others. If, however, you say, "People *sometimes* seem to be bored with my company," then you can begin to examine the differences in your behavior at times when others are bored versus the times they are not. Then you may choose whether you wish to behave in a way that will interest them. Discriminating thinking often leads to more functional outcomes than all-or-nothing thinking.

Personalized Thinking

Some people often assume responsibility for events over which they have no control. They may inappropriately take credit or blame for such events. They may misinterpret events as having significance for themselves, or they may interpret statements such as "I have a headache" as an implication that the other person doesn't like their company. When a coworker says she is putting in for a different job, they may interpret it to mean that she wants to get away from them. In its worst case, personalization may border on a kind of paranoia that comes from exaggerated self-reference.

Projective Thinking

Projective thinking is the opposite of personalization. Here people project the responsibility for their emotions and personal worth onto others. They may say, "I would have finished my college education if I had gotten more support from my wife." Or "I would have stopped smoking long ago if the people in my office weren't smokers." The projection of responsibility onto others is a cop out, a way of escaping responsibility for their own behavior.

Perfectionistic Thinking

Some people believe that nothing short of perfect performance is worthwhile. There is brittleness to such thinking. It actually may make success less likely. For example, if they break their diet one evening at dinner, they may conclude, "That's it! I might as well eat everything in sight. I haven't got the will power to diet properly." Their absolute standards make them vulnerable to discouragement. Alfred Adler recommended the courage to be imperfect for such persons.

Selective Abstraction

Here the tendency is to focus on a specific detail while ignoring the context. For example, you may overly respond to a hurried remark by a coworker without appreciating that she is under great pressure to complete a major task under an approaching deadline. In reviewing your work, your supervisor may have suggested improvement in one aspect of your performance after having mentioned many of your strengths. You may ignore the positive nature of the performance review and focus narrowly upon the suggested improvement. Because you discount the sea of positive comments by the supervisor, the one suggestion for improvement may loom like Mount Everest in your thinking.

Self-Punishing Thinking

The tendency to fault yourself irrationally robs you of energy and directs your attention away from your activities. While it is useful to acknowledge your shortcomings on the way to making improvements, it is self-defeating to fault yourself when the cause is unclear. Many people are their own worst critics. They seem ready to attack themselves any time events turn out badly. This self-punishing thinking creates a poor self-image, which in turn makes failure more likely. An example of such thinking is the tendency of older adults to attribute an occasional memory failure to the effects of aging. Younger people may experience similar lapses in memory without seeing the lapse as a symptom of dying brain cells. Cognitive scientists tell us that this tendency to explain memory lapses as a sign of old age worsens the problem. The fear that you will not be able to remember diverts your attention from the recovery of the memory, and the fear becomes a self-fulfilling prophecy.

Steps in Correcting Stressful Thinking

To correct your stressful thinking you must first become aware of it. Unfortunately, we are mostly *un*aware of what we are thinking while we are doing it. This works out all right most of the time. If, however, you have learned habitual patterns of inappropriate, stressful thinking, it is important to recognize them and to work to eliminate them. The following are suggestions for changing stressful thinking.

1. Practice listening to your self-talk when you feel stressful sensations. This will take considerable effort, as we are seldom accustomed to listening in on our internal monologues while we are stressed. This is the most important step, however, as no progress can be made in changing your thinking without first becoming aware of it.

2. Monitor your thinking for unrealistic assumptions that create stress. Do you find evidence of any of the stressful beliefs discussed earlier in this chapter? For instance, do you see yourself as a worthless person unless you are competent in all aspects of your life? Or, do you recognize that such a standard is rigid and unreasonable? Do you insist that others treat you considerately and fairly, and if at times they fail to do so, you label them as being bad people? Or, do you realize that from time to time we all allow our self-interests to blur our sense of fairness? Do you assume that you should always experience pleasure—that distasteful experiences are off-limits, any pain in your life unbearable? Or, do you understand that the "rain falls on the just and the unjust, that Rabbi Kushner (1981) was correct in observing that bad

things sometimes happen to good people?" Check your thinking for signs of these irrational beliefs and counter them with more functional statements.

3. Check also to see if you are processing information in a distorted manner. Are you exaggerating the seriousness of the situation or focusing narrowly on a single detail without considering its context? Are you engaging in all-or-nothing thinking—failing to appreciate degrees or shades of meaning? Are you either inappropriately personalizing the situation or projecting responsibility in order to escape your contribution to the stressful situation? Are you viewing the situation from a perfectionistic posture that is self-punishing and severely critical of others? Such cognitive distortions run so deep in our thinking that Beck (1976) refers to them as *automatic thoughts*. Consequently, it requires a great deal of careful scrutiny to recognize them.

4. Don't underestimate your coping resources for dealing with the stressful situation. Confidence in your resources is a great ally in confronting stressors. When you overestimate the gravity of the situation and underestimate your resources your giving yourself a vote of "no confidence."

5. Consciously use rational statements to counter irrational ones. For instance, if you are nervous in the presence of your boss, examine your thinking to discover thoughts that may be triggering or aggravating your nervousness. Counter these thoughts with objective statements such as, "There's rarely a problem with my work," or "Actually, I'm good at my job. There's no reason I should feel nervous."

6. Once you have examined your thinking for beliefs and perceptual distortions that may be contributing to your discomfort, take a second look at the actual situation. Focus on just the specifics, never mind the interpretation or explanation. Strive for a more objective understanding of what *actually* happened.

7. Identify alternative explanations for the stressful situation. Each alternative explanation must be at least as likely as the one that is causing you distress at the moment. For each of the alternatives ask yourself, "If I accepted this explanation, how would I feel?" Because all of the alternatives should be believable explanations for the situation, and since each leads to a differing emotional response on your part, remind yourself that you can choose how you wish to feel by your choice of an explanation.

8. Choose an alternative explanation that is less stressful than your original one and keep this explanation in mind whenever you think of the situation. Notice the difference in the way you feel.

Let's apply these steps to the following common experience. Bill has just received a test score from one of his instructors, and his reaction is highly self-punishing: "I flunked the damned exam! How stupid! No one who is as dumb as I am ought to be going to college anyway. Maybe I had better hang it up." This kind of talk is non-functional. It does not suggest constructive actions, and it is disheartening. This is clearly an example of exaggerated thinking. The results of one examination led Bill to conclude that he was stupid, dumb, and unable to measure up in college. He also engaged in self-punishing thinking. All this talk about being stupid and dumb misdirects his attention from the task. Such talk is unlikely to lead to constructive action, and to make matters worse, it is likely to injure his self-image.

Taking a second, more objective, look at the situation may suggest that Bill did *not* flunk the test at all. Sometimes a grade such as 75 or 80 is taken as failure, if self-expectations are extremely high. Perhaps Bill would conclude, on second look, that in reality he had made a C or B, and while this is below his expectations, it is hardly a failing grade.

Alternative explanations for his performance actually may be more reasonable than the one Bill had given himself. Perhaps it is not that he is "dumb," but that the exam was poorly written, or the instructor used an old and inappropriate examination. Or perhaps Bill did not study enough, or did not study the right topics. These alternative explanations will lead to different emotional responses. If he chooses to believe that the exam was poorly written he might turn self-deprecation into irritation toward the instructor for his slipshod work. If he chooses to believe that he had studied too little or inappropriately, then he can talk with others to see what he should have studied. This alternative may prove more helpful in coping with similar situations in the future than either of the others. After identifying alternative explanations, Bill should select the more promising of these and begin to take appropriate action.

In summary, irrational thinking creates a great deal of unnecessary stress. The process for eliminating such thinking involves taking a more realistic look at the troublesome situation, generating alternative explanations that are equally likely and taking action based on an alternative that leads to a constructive outcome and positive emotional response.

In this chapter we have reviewed approaches to overcoming stressful patterns of thinking through desensitization, thought suppression, the elimination of irrational self-talk and beliefs, and the correction of distorted perceptual processes. In the next chapter we will look at approaches for creating a stress-free consciousness.

Chapter 9

Creating Stress-Free Consciousness

How rarely I meet a man who can be free, even in thought! We all live according to rule. Some men are bed-ridden, all world-ridden.

—Henry David Thoreau

If your mind isn't crowded by unnecessary things, this is the best season of your life.

—Wu-Men

The approaches to overcoming stressful patterns of thinking discussed in the previous chapter are low-gear efforts compared to the approaches discussed in this chapter. Using a medical analogy, the approaches in chapter 8 are to the approaches in this chapter what conservative treatment is to surgery. Worn body joints may be managed conservatively with medication, heat, and exercise—or they may be replaced surgically. Conservative treatment in some cases only delays the inevitable. Joint replacement through surgery is more "radical," more invasive, but it may completely eliminate the problem. Approaches in this chapter are more global and pervasive, attacking the very roots of your consciousness. Instead of working on problems one by one, the consciousness disciplines attempt to change the entire mental set.

The key purpose for doing so is to enable you to act more consciously, deliberately, and preventively. It is far more desirable to bypass stressful experiences altogether than to be forced to confront them, no matter how successfully.

Stressful States of Consciousness

The consciousness of some people creates infernos of the mind. They suffer chronically from stressful states. Their conditioned way of viewing things creates negative emotional moods. Bullied by their feverish, pushy mental states, they suffer from a "scatterbrainedness" that diffuses their attention and weakens their efforts. Like nervous rats or hyperactive children they reflexively attend to whatever stimulates their senses. Their attention is directed first here and then there. They react rather than respond. They feel little control over their activities, and as a consequence, they approach the innumerable activities of their lives dutifully but resentfully. This trap is often referred to as the "tyranny of the trivial"—the idea that our daily lives can be consumed with a never-ending chain of meaningless tasks with only transitory meaning. These tasks, while sometimes important in the short run, can prevent us from attending to what is really important. Steven Covey (1989) listed the ability to create and pursue important long-range goals as one of the seven habits of highly effective people. Individuals who feel hopelessly trapped in trivial pursuits often long for more inner peace, more empowerment, and more freedom from their stressful conditioning. A metaphor for this type of thinking can be found in driver-education classes, where students are taught to fix their attention far enough ahead while driving that they can anticipate problems before they occur. Novice drivers sometimes focus their attention on what is happening directly in front of them. This shortsightedness prevents them from anticipating things before they happen. If you are only looking a few feet ahead, every stop sign, traffic light, and passing motorist is a surprise. You must react suddenly and dramatically.

Undisciplined Thinking

This scatterbrained approach to life is similar to electrical short-circuiting—crazy, high intensity energy that gets nothing done. St. Theresa in the Middle Ages referred to the undisciplined mind as an unbroken horse, and the sages of India referred to it as "a drunken monkey." This kind of consciousness leaves people feeling that their lives are out of control. They intuitively know that there is some more centered, composed state of consciousness to be experienced, but they feel cut off from it.

Such people are stuck within a punishing kind of consciousness that is out of sync with reality. It is as though they experience again and again punishing blows in a room with the lights turned off. They feel the pain but they can't identify the source of it. Lacking insight, they persevere in repeating the same failing efforts to free themselves. Voltaire once said, "Madness is doing the same thing over and over expecting different results." Stressful mind-sets are not creative mind-sets. How many times do you get trapped in a stressful situation with little insight? When you make incorrect assumptions about the nature of your distress, the assumptions lead to courses of action that make matters worse. The very things you are doing actually create additional problems. In this sense, the solution becomes a problem.

Cultural Consciousness

Entire cultures may participate in a consciousness that threatens their survival. One has only to travel back in history to the Nazi era in Germany for a perfect example. With notable exceptions, the mass of German people adopted a murderous worldview that doomed millions of supposedly inferior people to extinction and ultimately, like a boomerang, the violence came back to destroy their cities and to decimate their own population.

In *The Web of Life*, Fritjof Capra (1996) suggested that the most pressing problems of our time escape the understanding of the world's leaders. They fail to see the connection between the rampant poverty across much of the planet and the threat of overpopulation. They fail to see the connection between the extinction of animal and plant species on a massive scale and the burden of the massive debts owed by the countries in the Southern Hemisphere. And they fail to see the connection between inadequate resources, environmental degradation, and rapidly expanding populations on the one hand and the breakdown of local communities leading to ethnic and tribal violence that has become so visible in the post–cold war era. Capra maintains that there are solutions to such problems but that solutions would most likely require a radical shift in our cultural consciousness. In surveying the momentous problems facing modern peoples, John Lilly (1972) concluded, "It is my firm belief that the experience of higher states of consciousness is necessary for the survival of the human species."

The Psychology of Inner Experience

For most of this century American psychology had largely abandoned the study of consciousness and ignored the exploration of inner space. Out of its insecurity as a science, psychology identified with the experimental methods of the physical sciences. It was committed to logical positivism, a philosophy of science that asserts that no subject is worthy of investigation unless it can be studied via one of the five senses. If we cannot see it, hear it, feel it, smell it, or taste it, it does not exist for scientific purposes. With the growth of the human potential movement, and more recently of transpersonal psychology, however, this situation is changing. Once again, private experience is becoming a legitimate subject for investigation.

Rediscovery of the Religio-Philosophies of the East

The West is currently rediscovering the religio-philosophic practices of the East. Although certain trailblazers such as William James, Ralph Waldo Emerson, Henry David Thoreau, and Carl Jung attempted to translate these practices into Western frames, the richness of Eastern myth and methods has remained relatively obscure to most Americans. We were far too busy shaping and bending the external environment to share the concern of the East for the delicate nature of the internal environment. While the West was busy mastering the external world, the East was at work mastering the internal one. This gave them quite a head start toward the new spiritual frontier, the conquest of the inner world.

Consciousness Stabilizers

Charles Tart, a leading scientist within the consciousness disciplines, points out that when a certain conscious state is culturally endorsed, there are *stabilizers* set up to maintain it. Alternate ways of viewing reality are discouraged and concurrence with the standard version of reality is rewarded. Perhaps a more insidious form of indoctrination comes from the media. For example, many American spend several hours a day watching television, and they are saturated with slick advertising showing them what they should eat, drink, wear, drive, and do with their time. To a certain extent, such commercial messages can serve a purpose, but much of time they deliberately set very narrow standards for appearance, behavior, and attitudes. Whether culturally endorsed or not, any state of consciousness tends to persist.

The means by which models of reality are changed were discovered years ago by Canadian researchers with U.S. government funding. During the closing stages of the Korean War some American prisoners of war underwent brainwashing to turn them against their own government. In a broken down state they were filmed accusing the U.S. of imperialism and of high crimes. The resulting embarrassment prompted the government to investigate the brainwashing procedures after the war. The Canadians found that prolonged sensory deprivation loosened the person's sense of personal identity and personal values, rendering the person vulnerable to indoctrination. This was exactly the procedure used by the North Koreans to soften American POWs to the effects of communist propaganda.

Regulation of Stimulation Levels

It seems that your values and sense of identity are maintained by a constancy of stimulus input. We unconsciously strive to keep stimulation within a range that will maintain a kind of cognitive homeostasis. From experiments such as those conducted by the Canadians, a general principle was educed: *Anything that greatly decreases or increases one's basic level of stimulation for an extended period will make consciousness altering more likely*. It now appears that this principle can be used in changing your own consciousness. And because, for many, the consciousness they have created is bringing them much pain, the skillful use of this principle can be highly useful.

Practices that significantly increase stimulation, such as the whirling of Sufi dervishes or the running of a marathon, routinely alter people's consciousness. Part of the rewards of such practices is the tranquil, contented state they induce. A more common approach to consciousness altering, however, is the lowering of stimulation levels. By far, the most widely used nondrug practices for altering consciousness through the lowering of stimulation are meditation, yoga, and prayer—practices we will discuss in great detail later in this chapter.

The Consensual Trance

Consciousness is influenced strongly by both your past experiences and the consciousness of the culture you live in. Each culture casts a "reality" net over its members. The net represents the culture's views of what is and what should be. Members then operate under a consensual trance that seems to favor the survival of the culture more than the interests of its members. Because cultures are repositories of the values of its people, they are highly conservative and often resist updating. Thus cultural indoctrination, along with the effects of private experience, form an extensive set of beliefs about what is likely to happen. You filter your views of the present through these beliefs from the past, and they often become self-fulfilling prophecies. So consciousness in a sense creates your "reality." John Milton expressed it well in *Paradise Lost* when he wrote, "The mind is its own place and one can make a heaven of hell, a hell of heaven."

The Role of Religion in Challenging the Consensual Trance

Religious practices are designed to bring about a transformation of consciousness, to help us to awaken from the cultural trance. This elevated state of consciousness is referred to in the East as enlightenment, samadhi, or satori, and in Christian literature as being born again. In the New Testament we are admonished to challenge the consensual trance. "Be not conformed to the world," it says, "but be ye transformed by the renewing of your minds." This renewing of the mind is said to be unattainable "except ye become as a small child," that is, unless one achieves an innocence of perception stripped of conditioned artificiality. The basic goal of religious practice seems to be to help practitioners to climb above the clouded views of their contemporaries and to gain a more accurate view of what is. Religious mystics often report that from the vantage point of such elevated consciousness things look different, that the boundary between the observer and the object appears to blur, and that they feel a sense of oneness.

Such meta-views may bring people into conflict with the prevailing views of their cultures. Possessing an expanded awareness, they often challenge the narrowness of their cultures and are viewed as rebels. Jesus expresses this challenge to the existing paradigm when he said, "Ye have heard from them of old, but I say unto you . . ." Moses' vision challenged the conventional morality of the Egyptians and elicited the wrath of the Pharaoh. And Muhammad's challenge to the existing order triggered conflict with surrounding tribes.

At its best, the religious message seems to be to wake out of the consensual trance and to see things as they are, not as our models-of-how-the-world-is say they are. Regardless of the truth of its content, faith in a supernatural order seems to enhance your sense of happiness. Surveys generally demonstrate a low but consistent relationship between religious commitment and happiness (Csikszentmihalyi and Patton 1997; Myers 1993). At its worst, the message seems to be to discard the prevailing cultural view in favor of an alternative view of reality that is being recommended by a religious group. And perhaps worse yet, some religious traditions discourage questions regarding their versions of reality. Questioning religious authority is seen as hubris and is punished by ostracism or excommunication. Such traditions discount the individual experiences of their members as well as the advances of science. The resulting rigidity precludes needed updating of the traditional view of reality. The danger to devotees of such authoritarian systems can be seen in the fate of the Branch Davidians, members of the Heaven's Gate cult, and the followers of Jim Jones in British Guiana.

Fragmentation in Everyday Experience

Religious experience may reduce stress by overcoming the fragmented nature of human experience. Religious teaching throughout history has offered prescriptions for reconnecting, prescriptions for becoming whole again. Indeed, the word *religion* etymologically means to connect again or to bind back. The word *god* is used to represent that which has the highest significance for us humans. Religious teaching, then, is primarily concerned with leading us to experience union with the *significant* and thereby to rid ourselves of the stress that comes from estrangement, isolation, and loneliness. This prizing of unity or wholeness is shared by psychotherapy as well. Here the emphasis is on establishing integrity by unifying the forces within the personality.

Thinking vs. Awareness

Entrapment in a scaled-down version of reality is maintained in part by constant talking, talking to others or talking to yourself through thinking. It is difficult to listen when we are talking. Our awareness of what is happening is masked by our *thoughts about* what is happening. Consequently, if you want to tune in to what is happening, you must stop the incessant talking and still the mind with healing silence. Zen literature points up a basic incompatibility between thinking (talking to yourself) and awareness.

The Primacy of Awareness

Developmentally, awareness is primary, while thinking is secondary. In thinking you use categories. The use of categories becomes mental shorthand allowing you to process large quantities of observations economically. This shorthand is efficient. It allows you to communicate quickly with yourself and with others about a wide range of topics. But you engage in gross rounding off errors when you force objects and events into ready-made categories. These convenient categories form a little world inside of your head separate from the beautiful, ever-changing, real world which inexorably moves on. Meditation is a practice designed to help you break out of the reflexive self-perpetuating versions of reality and experience the present moment in all its richness.

Abstractions Increase with Age

As we grow older, more and more is demanded of us, and the use of these abstract categories becomes more and more important. Consequently, the original order of awareness and thinking becomes reversed: thinking now becomes primary, and awareness is reduced to a secondary function. You are aware of an object only long enough to see it as an instance of some category you have in mind. You may attend to the object only if it appears to have instrumental value for you in accomplishing your goals. In a sense you become prisoners of your mental conditioning, of your need to neatly categorize things. You become less open to new experiences. You are in touch with your environment only through preconceived, sometimes erroneous, impressions of it. Experiences become so routine, so automatic that you seldom feel vibrantly alive.

Past Conditioning Also Shapes Us

Past conditioning results in standard ways of viewing experience. The rapid, often careless, assignment of potentially new experiences to ready-made categories shuts you off to these new experiences. As a result, there is a predictable sameness to experiencing. All the uniqueness and freshness of the experience is lost in the rush to categorize it. Ken, for example, has been married to his wife, Mary, for nearly a half century. He often says he has no memories of life before marriage. Over the years a great deal of "entrainment" has occurred, that is, Ken's and Mary's interests have largely melded, and many of their values have become the same. Because they have shared so many experiences, they have such a long history, Ken imagines that he "knows" Mary. So much so, that he may not listen well, not fully hear her out. It seems like he doesn't have to, that he can anticipate what she is going to say. She begins her thought, and Ken, in his mind, completes her expression, thinking that he already has comprehended her message. If he's not careful, he doesn't respond to *her* but only to his *image* of her. The consciousness disciplines are designed to help you open up to present experience, to get beyond your biases, prejudices, and ready-made conclusions and experience the real.

Unless you challenge this lazy way of communicating, more and more experiences take on the quality of playbacks or reruns. We need to take our lives off automatic pilot, and as Thoreau said, to live *deliberately.* This approach requires significant changes in our consciousness. Three time-honored approaches appear particularly useful for elevating your consciousness: meditation, yoga, and prayer.

Meditation

Meditation has an ancient and venerable history in both Western and Eastern religious practice. Herbert Benson (1975), a medical researcher at Harvard University and author of *The Relaxation Response,* points out that meditation in one form or another was practiced by mystics of various religious persuasions. St. Augustine, Martin Luther, Fray Francisco de Osuna, St. Theresa, Father Nicolas, and other early Christian mystics practiced contemplation and recollection in order to shut off the mind from external thoughts and to produce a passive attitude and mental solitude. Contemplation or meditative exercises are also found in early Judaic literature. Merkabolism, the earliest form of mysticism in Judaism, involved repetition of a magic emblem. A thirteenth-century rabbi, Abulafia, used the letters of God's name as an object upon which to meditate. He also incorporated yogic breathing and body posture techniques. The Eastern meditative practices have been extremely influential. The best known is yoga meditation, the essence of which is concentration on a single point to achieve a passive attitude. Buddhism, Sufism, and Taoism, all primarily Eastern religions, contain many elements analogous to yoga meditation and thus to the relaxation response.

There is evidence that meditation practices were widespread among Jews throughout Jewish history. Students of the Kabbalah and Chasidic masters practiced meditation. Rabbi Aryeh Kaplan points out, "References to meditation are found in major Jewish texts in every period from the biblical to the premodern era (1985, p. 40)." He has written of this Jewish heritage in a series of books: *Meditation and the Bible, Meditation and the Kabbalah,* and *Jewish Meditation.*

Waking Up

Meditation is about waking up from a dream world. As we have discussed, we mistake our ideas *about* reality *for* reality. Because of strong needs and prejudices that lead to selective perception, some of the time we are dead wrong about what actually *is.* As we pointed out in the previous chapter, part of our thinking is flawed. We look out at the world through distorted perceptual processes. This faulty filtering of our experience creates a set of beliefs that often do not conform well to reality, and the consciousness formed from these beliefs creates stressful lifestyles.

Little Mind vs. Big Mind

We are often tyrannized by our needs, particularly conflicting needs. These tyrants can exhaust your energy and monopolize your attention. They cause you to look out at the world with selective perception, seeing only those things that have relevance for these needs. In the East, such a mental state is referred to as "little mind" in contrast to "big mind." When you get caught up with your egotistical goals, imprisoned within your "little mind," you miss much that is beautiful and ennobling in the world. With more fully developed consciousness, with "big mind," comes freedom from addictive demands and the opportunity to see things straight on. The big mind becomes a mirror to reflect reality without distortion. Such a nonattached, unaddicted, mirroring state of consciousness is similar to the pure consciousness that people are held to be capable of experiencing—so, attaining this meta-perspective (this *universal consciousness*) leads you to experience a sense of unity with all people (and, indeed, all things). Attaining this universal consciousness is said to create a sense of reality, control, and centeredness.

The work of meditation is to help you get in touch with reality, to break out of the dream or trancelike existence, to jettison stressful mind-sets, to free you from the punishing landscapes of your mind. While it is the nature of the mind to fly on automatic pilot and to miss the opportunity to live spontaneously, the mind also has the capacity to heal, to awaken you to the reality of present experience. The preferred method of millions for awakening is meditation.

Meditation Is a Practice

Meditation is not something you do over the weekend. Actually, there is no exact word among the Indian languages for the word *meditation*. The closest equivalent is a Pali word meaning "development through mental training (Kabat-Zinn 1994)." One does not train over a weekend but over a long time, and in the case of meditation perhaps over a lifetime. To make meditation work for you, you have to be ready for it. Like the Zen expression says, "When the pupil is ready, the teacher appears."

Focusing Attention

Old patterns of thought hold on stubbornly. The mind seems to have a mind of its own. Freud said, "Man is not even master in his own house, his own mind."

William James said the average person couldn't sustain attention for more than three seconds. Our streams of thought often seem illogical and incoherent. To see this for yourself, try the following experiments.

Experiment 1

Sit back quietly and for a few moments merely watch the stream of thoughts crossing your mind. Do not attempt to influence them, merely notice them.

Experiment 2

Now count backwards from 100, seeing each number clearly in your mind before going on to the next. It is unimportant how many numbers you cover during the minute. Your only goal is to sustain uninterrupted attention to the numbers. Once you become aware that your attention has wavered in the slightest from the task, stop the exercise. If your attention even briefly wanders to the question, "Has my attention wandered from the task?" you are through.

Usually participants in Experiment 1 indicate that their thoughts wandered badly over the time allotted. Moreover, they confess that there was little continuity to their thinking. Instead of a running narrative regarding some important topic, their thoughts were more like a jumble of old trinkets in an attic. One thing leads to another without logical connections. In Experiment 2 most participants find that their attention wanders from the task almost immediately. Can you imagine how much more effective we would be if we mastered our attention? If you were to spread twenty-five pounds of pressure across a chalkboard, you wouldn't even make a dent. If, however, you were to focus the pressure on the point of a diamond needle, you could easily pierce the board. Likewise, training in attention control leads to more effective living.

Although old patterns of thought tenaciously resist changing, dissatisfaction and pain often create a readiness for the change. You may sense something is terribly amiss about the way you are engaging things. You conclude that your life isn't working. At this point you may be ready to begin a practice that will help you escape your trance and confront reality head on, and meditation is just such a practice. Meditation attacks your neurotic views in two basic ways. It expands your awareness so you can experience the present moment and it breaks the grip of addictive needs that distort your grasp of reality.

Expanding Awareness Through Attention Training

Focused attention is highly empowering. In Hermann Hess's *Siddhartha*, once the Buddha had gained mastery over his attention, he was said to be amazingly effective in whatever he set out to do. Impressed by his accomplishments, others asked him for the secret of his success. He replied that whenever he set out to do anything he first prepared his mind through meditation, and then he would go after his purpose like a rock dropping through the water. Meditative practice is concerned with training our attention. Arthur Deikman (1974) says meditation *deautomatizes* your thinking. In other words, thinking may become so automatic that the behavior it governs is as reflexive as that of the bee or ant. In becoming more aware you become more choice-making.

To see how behavior and thinking can become automatic, consider the following questions: Can you identify the hidden rules that govern behavior at your work or in your family? What are the implied rules in your workplace that are never vocalized or written down? Consider for example the rule that meetings almost always occur in the office of the most important person. How about in your family? Are there unspoken rules such as, "When someone in the family becomes angry, family members are supposed to stop saying anything"? What are the rules that govern how you are to behave intimately toward a spouse or lover? What would change if these rules were verbalized?

Mindfulness meditation offers you freedom from the involuntary nature of much of your behavior. It further develops an internal witness to the stream of your consciousness. The resulting meta-perspective shrinks the gap between what you are doing and your awareness of what you are doing, ultimately giving you a greater sense of self-control. The meta-perspective taught by the great religio-philosophies is referred to by such expressions as "lifting the veil of Maya," "enlightenment," "being born again," "bare attention," and the like. In all of these traditions, some form of meditation is viewed as a royal route to consciousness expansion.

Staying in the Present

Meditation can also help you to be aware of the present moment. In *Walden*, Thoreau reminds us that, "Only that day dawns to which we are awake." Our awareness of the present is clouded so much of the time that we seldom are fully conscious of our experiences. When you set out to do one thing, you may be harassed by a multitude of "voice-overs"—little voices in your head reminding you of a thousand other things you have to do, or of the storm clouds gathering in your life, or of your failure to fulfill an obligation, or of myriad other thoughts that distract you from the present moment. Consequently, you may let the only *real* time you have pass unnoticed as you continue to live in your head. Many poets and writers of sacred literature have written about the importance of living in the present. The poet, Henry Wadsworth Longfellow, wrote:

> Trust no future, howe'er pleasant,
> Let the dead Past bury its dead!
> Act, act in the living Present!
> Heart within and God o'erhead.

Staying with your experiencing in the present moment implies faith in your coping abilities. To dodge present signals or to mentally rehearse future adjustments so completely that the future is shoved into the secure past is a vote of no confidence in your resources. To live in the present moment does not mean abandoning yourself to your impulses. To live in the present means avoiding the habit of endlessly processing fearful future events. Obviously, you need to have goals and make plans for the future. However, you shouldn't be so consumed with preparing for the journey that you miss the point of the journey in the first place.

Meditation Comes in Many Forms

There are many variations in the practice of meditation. Naranjo and Ornstein in *On the Psychology of Meditation* (1971) recount some of the different forms of meditation. Thus, while certain techniques (like those in the Tibetan Tantra) emphasize mental images, others discourage paying attention to any imagery; some involve sense organs and use visual forms (mandalas) or music, others emphasize a complete withdrawal from the senses; some call for complete inaction, and others involve action, gestures (mudra), walking, and other activities

Some ordinary experiences may create similar alterations in your consciousness as meditation. Sexual experiences or extreme sports such as skydiving or snowboarding serve as examples. Each of these creates a brief period in which you exist totally in the present moment and in which you break the automatic nature of your behavior and thinking. Such experiences are typically infrequent, however, and they seldom lead to lasting changes in consciousness. We speak of the *practice* of meditation for this reason. While a single experience of meditation may give a brief respite from a stressful mind-set, it takes the continual practice of the experience to effect lasting changes in your consciousness.

In whatever form, the practice of meditation has predictable physiological effects. Herbert Benson of Harvard Medical School and his colleague, J. Beary (1974), investigated the effects of various consciousness-altering experiences such as meditation, Zen, hatha yoga, sentic cycles, progressive relaxation, and hypnosis with suggested deep relaxation, and found all of them to elicit common physiological changes that contribute to optimal health. Among other changes, these practices decreased oxygen consumption, carbon dioxide production, muscle tension, breathing rate, heart rate, blood pressure, and metabolic rate, and they increased the production of alpha waves in the brain. All of these physiological changes are compatible with a lowering of nervous system activity and a state of deep relaxation and inner quietude.

Although the goals and effects of all forms of meditation are similar, the procedures for inducing a meditative state are quite different. Basically there are two categories of meditation: concentrative types and opening-up types. Whereas concentrative types attempt to narrow the focus of attention, opening up allows the mind to roam across a spectrum of stimulation. With opening-up types the goal is to strengthen your internal witness by merely being aware of whatever crosses your mind.

Concentrative Meditation

To meditate using concentrative forms is to dwell upon something. The goal is to focus attention on an object or experience such as your breath, a thought, a mantra, or spiritual passage to block out surrounding distractions and calm and center your mind. Zen masters referred to *single pointedness of attention* as one goal of such practice. The mind has a voracious appetite for stimulation. It is frenetically scanning the outer world for stimulation. If the external landscape is unstimulating, it turns to its own inner thoughts for stimulation. Because the mind demands stimulation, concentrative meditation is used to hook the mind on a single source of internal stimulation, and by endlessly repeating the source its meaning becomes less and less stimulating. The source becomes a kind of baffle to quiet the noisy internal environment and to expand your consciousness beyond the limited concerns.

In repeating the mantra, although you soon enough become habituated to it, you must still be paying enough attention to it for it to fully occupy the mind. Every thought is accompanied by weak muscle activity, that is, the thought causes limited firing of neurons that terminate in muscle tissue. The firing may not be enough to cause visible movements, but it does use energy, and it does involve muscle contraction. If you can preempt tension-arousing thoughts by tying up the mind with low-intensity stimulation, muscle tension is reduced, and profound relaxation takes over.

Common Elements in Concentrative Meditation

Although there are various forms of concentrative meditation, there are elements common to all of them. Whatever form of meditation you choose, use the following guidelines.

Proper setting.

Choose a quiet room with a moderate temperature. Sit in a padded straight-back chair, preferably without arms. Place your feet flat on the floor, approximately shoulder-width apart, and lay hands comfortably on your thighs. Keep the top of your head parallel with the ceiling. Do not cross either your arms or legs. This position should prove comfortable and should activate as few muscles as possible.

Focusing attention on a limited source of stimulation.

Because your goal is to stop or slow the frenetic pace of your thinking, you should narrow the focus of your attention. You could focus your attention on a visual figure such as a mandala (a figure that captures one's attention) or a sound such as a mantra. Most people will find it easier to focus upon a sound than on a visual figure. Because you will make the sound inaudibly, you should choose a sound that is easy to hear in your mind. Usually sounds that have one or more of the following consonants prove useful for this purpose: "m," "n," "ng," or "h." Sounds using these consonants tend to resonate and are more easily remembered. To see what we mean, place your fingers on your cheekbones and say "Aum." Now, "aing," and then, "humm." Did you feel a resonance in your cheekbones? Now with your fingers still on your cheekbones, say Coca-Cola. What happened to the resonance?

If you choose to focus on your breath instead of a mantra, either note the air coming down and out of your throat like a swinging door, or concentrate on the expansion and contraction of your stomach with each breath. You also might choose a spiritual passage from the sacred literature of your faith as your focus. The Russian Orthodox Church urges its followers throughout the day to recite the Jesus Prayer: "Lord Jesus, have mercy upon us sinners." Roman Catholics are urged to recite the Hail Mary prayer. Protestants may use the Lord's Prayer.

Repeat the source of stimulation continuously.

When any source of stimulation becomes repetitive enough, the brain accommodates to it to decrease its disproportionate reaction to it. The phenomenon is called sensory accommodation. Consequently, as the source is repeated over and over, its ability to excite the brain is increasingly reduced. What is left is a mind hooked on a source of stimulation that has little stimulation value. This practice then eliminates the stressfulness of our thinking and returns us to the quietness of our center.

Resist the temptation to evaluate the experience.

Perhaps the most important ingredient in the formula for inducing the meditative state is a passive attitude. You must let go, go negative, not try. The Zen masters advise, "Gentle is the way." Do not fight extraneous thoughts. If your mind wanders, merely return to the silent repetition of the mantra. Very often, beginners complain that they are unable to keep their attention focused on the mantra. If this happens to you, merely be aware of your wandering thoughts and gently bring your attention back to the mantra. Daniel Goleman (1971) suggests a positive way to view wandering thoughts. According to him, there may be a kind of built-in relaxostat that makes us aware of wandering thoughts when they threaten to disturb a state of relaxation. If this is the case, the mind wandering during meditation may actually desensitize you to anxious thoughts by associating them with the feeling of deep relaxation.

Approve of the altered mind-set.

Another crucial element of concentrative meditation is to begin with an accepting attitude. It is important that you understand the benefits to be derived from the practice. Do not be turned off to the practice by others who maintain that meditation is an occult practice that might weaken your faith. Earlier we have referred to the use of meditation by all of the great religious traditions. Meditation is neutral in respect to theology. It is a mental discipline that allows you to escape the narrow vision of your mind. It creates a freshness to your experience and allows you to gain a clearer grasp of reality.

Opening-Up Meditation

Opening-up meditation is usually referred to as *mindfulness* meditation. Its goal is a heightened awareness of thought and action. Its emphasis is on strengthening the witness and in living in the present.

The Witness

Mindfulness meditation fosters a dual consciousness. That is, one level of consciousness observing another level of consciousness. Have you ever had a distressing dream in which you comforted yourself by saying something like, "Don't worry. This is just a dream. You'll wake up and everything will be okay"? You see, one level of consciousness is tuning in on yet another. In the East this meta-level is referred to as the *spectator* or the *witness*.

The Western cognitive sciences have a similar concept. They refer to meta-cognition, that is, thought about thought. Mindfulness meditation strengthens this kind of meta-cognition, expands your awareness of what you are doing *while you are doing it*. This is the key. If you know what you are doing and why you are doing it while you are doing it, you will be less likely to be stressed by what you are doing or to *become* stressed because of something you've done. By being mindful of your actions you are free, if necessary, to change your behavior before you do any damage, thus avoiding unnecessary stressful encounters.

Practicing Mindfulness

Preparation for mindfulness meditation is in part the same as for concentrative forms. It is helpful to create a proper setting for the practice. This usually involves a quiet room, a comfortable chair, and a relatively straight sitting posture with the arms and legs uncrossed. As with concentrative forms, you should not evaluative the experience and you should hold a positive attitude regarding the value of the experience.

Mindfulness meditation differs from the concentrative forms in that it does *not* attempt to focus attention on a single source of stimulation. With mindfulness you merely follow your attention without trying to direct it. The real purpose of mindfulness is to strengthen the witness by observing what you are doing and thinking while you are doing so. The content of your thinking is unimportant. You merely sit and observe whatever comes to mind. You are learning to pay attention moment to moment instead of focusing on the past or future

This may sound like a worthless practice, letting the mind wander capriciously. However, there is a discipline to the experience. You are attempting to maintain a dual consciousness. And strangely enough, this seeming laissez-faire approach contributes greatly to a sense of self-control. The Japanese roshi Shunryu Suzuki (1970) said, "To give your sheep or cow a large, spacious meadow is the way to control him (p. 31)." The expanded awareness created by a more active witness allows you to make choices and causes you to feel more control over your life.

There is another sense in which mindfulness increases your sense of control. As you become aware of what you are thinking, the thinking itself tends to cease. It's like shining a light into a dark room. As the light comes in, the darkness vanishes. So you sit quietly and merely monitor your thoughts. You may begin to think of a bill that's unpaid. You observe the thought *without trying to stop it*, and the thought tends to melt away. Next, you wonder how long you have been meditating. Again, you focus attention on the thought, and it too fades. You continue the process and your mind becomes emptied, quiet, and calm like the surface of a lake. Like the lake, your mind becomes a mirror reflecting *what is* without distortion.

The benefit of mindfulness meditation is both immediate and long term. The immediate benefit is the reduction of stress and the relaxed, contented feeling state it induces. The long-term benefit from the regular practice of mindfulness is the increased awareness of what you are doing while you are doing it. As we indicated earlier, typically there is a gap between the time you do or think something and your awareness of it. Mindfulness, with the strengthening of the witness, greatly decreases the gap so that you are more immediately aware. Being aware of what you are doing at the moment allows you to avoid many stressful conflicts and saves a great deal of energy.

Active Meditation

It is a mistake to think that you can meditate only when you are in a certain meditative situation. Any activity can serve to train the witness. You can exercise the witness while you are driving the car or writing a letter or cooking a meal. All you have to do is be aware of what you are doing while you are doing it. Gary Snyder (1990, p. 23) put it well:

> Changing the filter, wiping noses, going to meetings, picking up around the house, washing dishes, checking the dipstick—don't let yourself think these are distracting you from your more serious pursuits. Such a round of chores is not a set of difficulties we hope to escape from so that we may do our "practice" which will put us on a "path"—it *is* our path.

Yoga

Yoga is a Sanskrit word meaning yoking or uniting. Although yoga is a system of self-development that takes many forms, the form most commonly practiced by Westerners is *hatha yoga*. Hatha yoga combines gentle stretches, breathing, and meditation to strengthen the body and to calm the mind. One assumes gentle stretches, called *asanas*, for brief periods. These stretches increase muscle flexibility. One of the effects of stress is to increase muscle tightness. These yogic stretches help reduce the effects of stress by loosening the muscles. Yogic breathing also alleviates the stress response by changing the balance between oxygen and carbon dioxide in the blood. This change in blood chemistry increases parasympathetic nervous system activity that, in turn, triggers the relaxation response.

Assuming the yogic postures becomes a meditation if you focus your attention moment by moment on the sensations caused by the stretching. You should attend to the sensations of the muscles caused by the stretching. For this purpose, it doesn't matter whether you are able to stretch as far as the next person can. What really counts is whether you are able to discipline the mind, to master your attention, to break the control of your conditioned thinking. The Hindu swami Patanjali around 150 B.C., wrote: "Yoga is the stopping of the spontaneous [think conditioned] activities of the mind."

If you choose to seriously practice hatha yoga, you would do well to enroll for a yoga class in your community. Many universities, civic groups, and some churches and synagogues offer yoga courses. You will make progress much faster with the assistance of an experienced yoga teacher. Otherwise, you might wish to purchase a yogic text like Richard Hittleman's (1969) *Yoga: Twenty-Eight Day Exercise Plan*. Such texts often contain pictures of the yogic postures and give complete instructions for each. To get a feel for the experience, however, you might try the following postures. To prepare for them you should wear loose clothing with shoes removed. Practice the postures on a mat on the floor. Remember that the goal is to keep your mind on your muscles to break out of your conditioned thinking.

Chest Expansion

With your feet separated about a fist's width and your arms dangling loosely at your sides, stand quietly for a moment to center down. Slowly lift your arms to the side and swing them forward until the backs of your hands are together. Then swing them backward until they meet, and clasp your hands together. Next, tilt your head back while you raise your arms to a point of tension but not pain. Hold a position creating a comfortable tension for about ten seconds. With your arms still lifted, tilt your body forward until you feel stretching but without pain. Hold the farthest position for about twenty seconds. Now, slowly raise your body as though you were uncoiling until you are standing upright. Release your arms and allow them to once again dangle loosely at your sides. Remain in this resting position for approximately one minute while you continue to feel the warm, stretching sensations primarily in your chest, arms, and small of your back. You may consider yourself to have succeeded if you were able to keep your attention glued on the sensations of your muscles throughout the experience.

Side Tilt

Stand upright with arms dangling at your sides. Spread your feet a little wider. Slowly raise your arms out to your sides to shoulder height. Tilt your body to the left until your left arm touches your left leg. While doing so, bring your right arm over your head toward your left side. Slide your left arm down your left leg as far as you comfortably can while continuing to bring your right arm farther to the left side. When you reach the farthest point that doesn't trigger pain, hold the position for twenty seconds. Then slowly right the body keeping the arms outstretched like a windmill. Continue tilting to the right until you slide your right arm as far as you comfortably can down your right leg. As before, continue bringing the left arm over the head as far as possible. Hold this position for twenty seconds also. Once again right your body and stand with your arms at your sides for one minute.

Prayer

Many people find stress relief in prayer. In some polls as many as ninety percent of Americans say they believe in God, and almost as many say they pray from time to time. Prayer is the act of communicating with a higher power. Some experts say it doesn't matter whether you address a specific deity (such as God or Allah) or just an unknown force in the universe. According to Larry Dossey, M.D., (1993) author of *Healing Words*, the act of relying on a force more powerful than yourself gives you a sense of confidence that you don't have to handle your problems alone. The prayer may be a ritualized one like the Lord's Prayer or the Hail Mary prayer or it may be a spontaneous utterance.

As we discussed, the repeated recitation of prayers such as the Hail Mary of the Roman Catholics or the Jesus Prayer of the Russian Orthodox Church can have many of the benefits of concentrative meditation.

Larry Dossey (1993) offers three prescriptions for those who are beginning the practice of prayer:

- Keep it simple. By this he means that neither the words used nor the form of the prayer is important. What is important is that you sincerely attempt to make contact with a power outside yourself.

- Start small. He suggests that perhaps just waking up in the morning and saying a simple thank-you may be a good beginning—or perhaps beginning with an expression of appreciation before meals.

- Don't focus on relief. While prayer may offer you great relief and may improve your health, it is less likely to do so if this is the focus of your prayer. This advice is reminiscent of the Zen saying regarding meditation, "Entertain no gaining idea." Stress relief should be seen as secondary to the practice.

Whether you choose meditation, yoga, prayer, or another technique, these practices have the ability to awaken, heal, and to help you overcome stressful patterns of thinking. Remember that these are disciplines, not instant or overnight panaceas. The commitment to practice one or more or these techniques on a daily basis, however, can transform your consciousness and open the door to a fuller, stress-free existence.

Chapter 10

Putting It All Together

Difficulties are meant to rouse, not discourage.

—William Ellery Channing

Coping with stress is a lifelong task. Every day that you are alive is a day that you will be challenged to cope with life demands. It is impossible, however, to find a single cure for stress: life is just too complex and dynamic to be reduced to a few simple techniques that will magically cure stress. However, some approaches for handling stress work better than others, and in this concluding chapter we provide a systematic plan for coping with stress that draws on the material covered throughout this book. Recommendations are arranged into two sections: recommendations for preventive coping and recommendations for combating stressors once they are engaged.

Preventive Coping

Successful coping begins with prevention. Time spent in preventing stressors is more cost-effective than time spent in combating them. Avoiding as many stressors as possible through careful planning and decision-making is the key for living healthfully. Much of the information we presented in the second half of this book—the material on developing coping resources in chapter 6, the information about stress and personality covered in chapter 7, and the suggestions for overcoming stressful patterns of thinking as well creating stress-free consciousness in chapters 8 and 9—can be used for prevention of stress. Look for ways to develop resources before you need them—for example, by developing social networks and engaging in health-promoting activities like proper nutrition and exercise.

Pay careful attention to your results from the self-assessment of coping resources presented in chapter 6. Having adequate coping resources creates a general resistance to stress. People rich in coping resources are seldom intimidated by life's demands. They size up the demand, apply their resources, and are energized by the experience. People with deficient resources, however, often respond with shrinking timidity. They frequently feel overwhelmed by life's demands and approach new experiences with fear and hesitation. If your self-assessment revealed inadequacies in your stock of coping resources, you should work especially hard at developing them using the techniques in later chapters.

It is wise to work to strengthen your resources during periods in which life demands have lightened. The Social Readjustment Rating Scale in chapter 4 measures your current demands. If your score on the scale revealed that you are currently under a great deal of stress, implement your resource-building techniques in a slow, step-by-step fashion. Otherwise your attempts to cope could begin to feel like one more overwhelming stressor in your life. Just as the moon waxes and wanes or the tides rise and fall, life demands are also constantly shifting. All of us can count on certain times when we have more breathing room in handling life demands. During these periods of low stress you can enrich your armory of coping resources so that you will feel more empowered when confronting future demands. Focus especially on the following recommendations to develop your preventive coping resources.

Practice Wellness

Wellness is a highly energized state of physical and mental well-being that provides you with an abundance of energy for meeting challenging situations. Each of the resources inventoried in chapter 6 can be an important component of wellness. Virtually all demands prove stressful if you are overextended and fatigued. Exercise and rest create the energy you need to cope well.

- *Take up aerobic exercise.* Aerobic exercise is the closest thing to a panacea for life's ills. Among other benefits, it burns up stress hormones, lowers blood pressure, prevents heart disease, decreases the chances of osteoporosis, helps regulate weight, and greatly increases your energy reserves. Unfortunately, it requires self-discipline and, as a result, most people do far too little of it. Even a few minutes of exercise each day, however, will yield a cornucopia of benefits that will significantly improve the quality of your life.

- *Get good rest.* Adequate rest is a close second to exercise as a means of preventing stress, and sleep is the best way to get it. You need deep sleep for physiological recuperation, and dream sleep to release stressful states and to improve mental functioning. Experts warn that if you are seriously sleep-deprived, you are pushing your body to the limit without providing for the recharging of your batteries. Most people require seven to eight hours of uninterrupted sleep for optimal functioning, but studies suggest that the average person gets less.

Practice Thought Control

As we discussed in chapters 8 and 9, your thinking creates much of your stress. Your beliefs and self-statements reflect your past experiences. Most of them are quite functional; some, however, are self-defeating. These beliefs are so deeply engrained that you may not recognize their powerful influence on your moods and behavior. Some negative beliefs discount your personal worth, some represent the motives of other people as being generally malicious, and some represent the normal conditions of life as threatening. Look behind your thoughts to the beliefs that prompt them. Challenge the reality of these beliefs. Ask yourself, "Is this true?" Often you will find that you have constructed a private kind of logic that doesn't accord with reality.

Deepen Your Spiritual Life

We are so busy *doing* and *having* that we often neglect *being*. We allow ourselves to be tyrannized by immediate and sometimes trivial concerns. As a consequence, life becomes shallow and more vulnerable to stress. A serene state of consciousness is a powerful resource when confronting situations that typically stress you. Many different paths lead to a rich interior life. Millions follow the practices of one of the great religious traditions. Some people have trouble conforming to the belief systems of institutional religion and create more personal paths. Whichever path is followed, spiritual practice brings meaning and a broader sense of identity.

Practice Relaxation Daily

As we have suggested at several points in this book, it is important to take time to relax each day. We have inherited a nervous system that is hypersensitive to potential threat or loss. It is like a wild beast that nervously reacts to everything around it. High states of arousal militate against healthy adjustment. You must practice methods of taming the nervous system, of returning it to quiescence. At least once or twice each day, take time to decompress, to de-escalate through relaxation. There are many effective ways of relaxing. For many people music will work like magic to calm the troubled mind. Some find a quiet walk will do the trick. Others turn to hobbies such as gardening. Still others use formal methods of relaxing, such as prescribed breathing, the quieting response, deep muscle relaxation, the relaxation response, alpha training, or prayer.

Combative Coping

Once you are caught up in a stressful situation or are facing a stressful event, it is time to make use of your coping resources. If you possess a rich set of resources, your stress arousal will be less intense and its duration will be significantly shorter. We covered some of your options for combating stressors in chapter 5, but the following steps for using your resources in coping with stressors will serve as a helpful guide.

Step 1: Prepare Yourself

Once you have become aware of the stressor, attempt to prepare yourself to handle it more efficiently. A few minutes of preparation may help you to think more objectively about the situation and may contribute to a greater sense of control. Control your thinking. Your body takes its cues from your thinking. It initiates stressful reactions only when your mind sounds an alarm. Stress is not an objective reality! It is not something "out there." It is a function of your perception, and therefore you have control over it. So, curb the tendency to exaggerate the seriousness of the situation and to discount the adequacy of your resources for coping with it.

Step 2: Stay in the Present

Bring your thoughts back into the present by centering your attention on your breathing, some sound or visual pattern that invites attention, some repetitive movement, or some prayer. The present is seldom very stressful. What is stressful is the future with its worries about what could happen or the past with its thoughts about what should have happened.

Step 3: Get a Clear Reading on the Stressor

Some stressors have a serious impact but are difficult to bring into sharp focus. You may sense danger or impending loss while the outline of the stressor remains faint and ill defined. You may try to ignore it because thinking about it distresses you. Just as it is difficult to hit a moving target, it is difficult to take effective action against stressors that are poorly understood. As we suggested in chapter 4, the first step in effective coping is to get a better reading on the stressor, to bring it more clearly into focus. Face rather than ignore the stressor; seek additional information from others. Ask yourself "What am I in for?" and "How can I best handle it?"

Step 4: Inventory Your Coping Resources

It is not only important to *have* resources, it is also important to *acknowledge* them, which was the point of the coping resources inventory offered in chapter 6. Many people who are reasonably endowed with resources still approach difficult circumstances from a fearful stance. Their attention is dominated by the stressful situation, and they fail to appreciate the resources they possess.

- Ask yourself, "What would I need in order to successfully cope with this situation?" and note how many of the necessary skills and resources you already possess. Spend considerable time thinking about these resources.

- Remind yourself of past successes in dealing with other stressful life situations. Relive significant aspects of these situations in which you demonstrated the adequacy of your resources. Visualize yourself once again successfully handling the stressful situation. Remind yourself that you managed the stressor quite well in these situations even though at the time it was not immediately obvious how you were to do it. Give yourself credit for being a good coper.

- Remember the road map for stress presented in chapter 3— spend at least half as much time inventorying your resources as you spend evaluating the stressor. Confidence is a valuable ally in combating stress, and confidence builds on memories of past successes.

Step 5: Decide Whether the Stressor Is Controllable or Uncontrollable

If the situation is controllable, commit yourself to some reasonable course of action in dealing with the stressor. Action is itself a powerful stress-reducer. Research shows that when you shift into action, the body *lowers* its production of a powerful stress hormone, epinephrine. Therefore, any action you take will lessen the stress initially. Later, however, the value of the action as a stress-reducer will depend on its appropriateness.

- Don't avoid taking action out of fear of making the wrong decision. Remind yourself that there are many different ways of successfully dealing with a stressful situation. Often you make a decision, and then make it the *right* decision by working at it. Obviously, we don't mean for you to take an impatient, impulsive approach to stressful situations. We *do* mean to encourage you to take action once you have reasonably researched the problem.

- Remind yourself that you will never know whether the decision is correct until after you have made it. You may have a pretty good idea as to its merits, but proof can only be seen once the consequences of the decision become apparent.

- Congratulate yourself for taking action, for being resolute. A positive mood will energize you for more effective action against stressors, and self-endorsement contributes significantly to upbeat mood states.

- Be open to negative feedback regarding the appropriateness of your action. Even the most studious research of a problem will sometimes lead to inappropriate courses of action. Now and then it will become necessary to step back and adopt a different course of action.

If the situation is uncontrollable, direct your coping efforts to the control of your emotions. Timely action at this point will prevent emotional hijacking that will creating ever-greater stressful arousal.

- Reframe the situation to look for positive elements that might make the experience less stressful. One promising tack is to ask, "What can I learn from this situation?"

- Resist the tendency to make matters worse by exaggerating the threat posed by the stressor.

- Body scan to monitor stressful arousal and use relaxation procedures such as regulated breathing, deep muscle relaxation, or the relaxation response to cool down.

In conclusion, comprehensive stress management includes both preventive and combative coping. Successful coping requires the building of resources, and this takes extended effort. Be wary of advertisers who spend billions of dollars trying to convince you that the solutions to life's problems rest with the purchase of a product, drug, or service. In the end, the work of successful coping pays rich dividends. It leaves you with a greater sense of control over your life which, in turn, elevates your sense of self-esteem and energizes you for more vibrant living.

References

Aldwin, C. M. 1994. Does age affect the stress and coping process? Implications of sex differences in perceived control. *Journal of Gerontology* 46:174–180.

American Heart Association. *Heart and Stroke Facts: 1996 Statistical Supplement.* 1996. Dallas: American Heart Association.

Amundson, M. E., C. A. Hart, and T. H. Holmes. 1981. *Manual for the Schedule of Recent Experience.* Seattle: University of Washington School of Medicine.

Anthony, D., B. Ecker, and K. Wilber, eds. 1987. *Spiritual Choices: The Problems of Recognizing Authentic Paths to Inner Transformations.* New York: Paragon House.

Antoni, M. H. 1987. Neuroendocrine influences in psychoimmunology and neoplasia: A review. *Psychology and Health* 1:3–24.

Antonovsky, A. 1979. *Health, Stress and Coping.* San Francisco: Jossey-Bass.

Ardell, D. 1977. *High-Level Wellness*. Emmaus, Penn.: Rodale Press.

Bandura, A. 1982. Self-efficacy mechanism in human agency. *American Psychologist* 37(2):137–144.

Barnett, R. C., and C. Rivers. 1996. *She Works, He Works*. San Francisco: Harper.

Beary, J., and H. Benson. 1974. Common effects of conscious-altering procedures. *Psychosomatic Medicine* 36(2):154–165.

Beck, A. T. 1976. *Cognitive Therapy and the Emotional Disorders*. New York: International Universities Press.

Ben-Porath, Y. S., and A. Tellegen. 1990. A place for traits in stress research. *Psychological Inquiry* 1:14–40.

Benson, H. 1975. *The Relaxation Response*. New York: William Morrow.

———. 1984. *Beyond the Relaxation Response*. New York: Berkley.

Brickman, P., D. Coates, and R. Janoff-Bulman. 1978. Lottery winners and accident victims: Is happiness relative? *Journal of Personality and Social Psychology* 36:917–927.

Brown, J. D., and K. L. McGill. 1988. The high cost of success. Paper presented at the American Psychological Association Convention, Atlanta, Ga.

Brown, L. 1993. A prayer a day. *American Health*, March, 27.

Cabell, J. B. 1926. *The Silver Stallion*. London: J. Lane.

Cannon, W. B. 1932. *The Wisdom of the Body*. New York: W. W. Norton.

———. 1936. The role of emotion in disease. *Annals of Internal Medicine* 9(2):145–160.

Capra, Fritjof. 1996. *The Web of Life*. New York: Anchor Books, Doubleday.

Castenada, C. 1972. *A Separate Reality*. New York: Pockett Books.

Charles, C. L. 1999. *Why Is Everyone So Cranky?*. New York: Hyperion.

Chicago Tribune. 1987. Rich think big about living well. September 24, p. 3.

Cohl, H. A. 1997. *Are We Scaring Ourselves to Death?* New York: St. Martin's Griffin.

Cooley, C. H. 1902. *Human Nature and the Social Order*. New York: Schocken Books.

Cousins, N. 1983. *The Healing Heart*. New York: Norton.

Covey, S. 1989. *The Seven Habits of Highly Effective People*. New York: Simon and Schuster.

Csikszentmihalyi, M. 1990. *Flow*. New York: Harper and Row.

————. 1999. If we are so rich, why aren't we happy? *American Psychologist* 54(10):821–827.

Csikszentmihalyi, M., and J. D. Patton. 1997. Happiness, the optimal experience, and spiritual values: An empirical study of adolescents. *Revue Quebecoise do Psychologie* 18:167–190.

Deal, S. L., and J. E. Williams. 1988. Cognitive distortions as mediators between life stress and depression in adolescents. *Adolescence* 23(90):477–490.

Deikman, A. J. 1974. Deautomatization and the mystic experience. In *The Nature of Human Consciousness*, edited by R. E. Ornstein. New York: The Viking Press.

Dembroski, T. J., J. M. MacDougall, R. B. Williams, T. L. Haney, and J. A. Blumenthal. 1985. Components of type A, hostility, and anger-in: Relationship to angiographic findings. *Psychosomatic Medicine* 47(3):219–232.

Dement, W. C. 1999. *The Promise of Sleep*. New York: Random House.

Dominguez, J., and V. Robin. 1993. *Your Money or Your Life: Transforming Your Relationship with Money and Achieving Financial Independence*. New York: Penguin.

Dossey, L. 1993. *Healing Words: The Power of Prayer and the Practice of Medicine*. San Francisco: Harper.

Dudley, D., and E. Welke. 1977. *How to Survive Being Alive*. New York: Doubleday.

Elliott, R. S. 1986. Cognitive and behavioral stress management considerations. A presentation to the American College of Cardiology. Jackson Hole, Wyoming. July.

Ellis, A. 1981. *Rational Emotive Therapy and Cognitive Behavior Therapy*. New York: Springer.

————. 1973. The no cop-out therapy. *Psychology Today*, July, 56–62.

Engebretson, T., and K. Matthews. 1992. Dimensions of hostility in men, women, and boys: Relationships to personality and cardiovascular responses to stress. *Psychosomatic Medicine* 54(3): 311–323.

Farley, F. 1986. The big T in personality. *Psychology Today* April, 44–52.

Fowler, J. 1981. *Stages of Faith*. San Francisco: Harper and Row.

Frank, R. H., and P. J. Cook. 1995. *The Winner-Take-All Society*. New York: Simon and Schuster.

Freudenberger, H. J. 1974. Staff burnout. *Journal of Social Issues* 30(1): 159–165.

Friedman, H. S., and S. Booth-Kewley. 1987. The "disease prone personality": A meta-analytic view of the construct. *American Psychologist* 42(6):539–555.

Friedman, H. S., J. S. Tucker, J. E. Schwartz, C. Tomlinson-Keasey, L. R. Martin, D. L. Wingard, and M. H. Criqui. 1975. Psychosocial and behavioral predictors of longevity. *American Psychologist* 50 (2):69–78.

Friedman, M., and R. H. Rosenman. 1974. *The Type A Personality and Your Heart.* Greenwich, Conn.: Fawcett Publications.

Gazzaniga, M. S. 1988. *Mind Matters.* Boston: Houghton Mifflin.

Girdano, D. A., G. S. Everly, and D. E. Dusek. 1997. *Controlling Stress and Tension,* 5th ed. Boston: Allyn and Bacon.

Glass, D., R. Contrada, and G. Snow. 1972. Stress, type A behavior, and coronary disease. *Weekly Psychology Update* 1(1):5–9.

Glass, D. C., and J. Singer. 1972. *Urban Stress.* New York: Academic Press.

Gleick, J. 1999. *Faster.* New York: Pantheon.

Goleman, D. 1971. Meditation helps break the stress spiral. *Psychology Today*, February, 4–6.

———. 1994. *Emotional Intelligence.* New York: Bantam Books.

Greenberg, J. S. 1999. *Comprehensive Stress Management,* 6th ed. Boston: McGraw Hill.

Grossarth-Maticek, R., I. Bastiaans, and D. T. Kanazir. 1985. Psychosocial factors as strong predictors of mortality from cancer, ischaemic heart disease and stroke: The Yugoslav prospective study. *Journal of Psychosomatic Research* 29:167–176.

Hayflick, L. 1994. *How and Why We Age.* New York: Ballantine Books.

Hesse, H. 1961. *Siddhartha.* New York: New Directions.

Hittleman, R. 1969. *Yoga.* New York: Bantam Books.

Hobfoll, S. E. 1989. Conservation of resources: A new attempt at conceptualizing stress. *American Psychologist* 44(3):513–524.

Holmes, T. H., and R. H. Rahe. 1967. The social readjustment rating scale. *Journal of Psychosomatic Research* 11:213–218.

Johnson, C. L. 1998. Emotional strategies in adapting to long-term survivorship. In M. H. Silver, chair, Personality and longevity: Is who we are related to how long we live? Symposium accepted for the 51st Annual Scientific Meeting of the Gerontological Society of America. Philadelphia, Penn.

Joy, W. B. 1969. *Joy's Way.* Los Angeles: Jeremy P. Tarcher.

Justice, B. 1988. *Who Gets Sick.* Los Angeles: Jeremy P. Tarcher.

Kabat-Zinn, J. 1994. *Wherever You Go There You Are.* New York: Hyperion.

Kanner, A. D., J. C. Coyne, C. Schaefer, and R. D. Lazarus. 1981. Comparison of two modes of stress measurement: Daily hassles and uplifts versus major life events. *Journal of Behavioral Medicine* 4:1–39.

Kaplan, A. 1985. *Jewish Meditation.* New York: Schocken Books.

Kegan, R. 1994. *In Over Our Heads.* Cambridge: Harvard University Press.

Kobassa, S. C. 1979. Stressful life events, personality, and health: An inquiry into hardiness. *Journal of Personality and Social Psychology* 37:1–11.

Krohne, H. W. 1990. Personality as a mediator between objective events and their subjective representation. *Psychological Inquiry* 1:260–29.

Krugman, P. R. 1992. Disparity and despair. *U. S. News and World Report,* March 23, 54.

Kushner, H. S. 1981. *When Bad Things Happen to Good People.* New York: Schocken Books.

Laudan, L. 1994. *The Book of Risks.* New York: Wiley.

Lazarus, R. S. 1966. *Psychological Stress and the Coping Process.* New York: McGraw-Hill.

———. 1981. Little hassles can be hazardous to your health. *Psychology Today,* July, 58–62.

———. 1981. The stress and coping paradigm. In *Models of Clinical Psychopathology,* edited by C. Eisdorfer, D. Cohen, A. Kleinman, and P. Maxim. New York: Spectrum.

Lazarus, R. S., and S. Folkman. 1984. *Stress, Appraisal, and Coping.* New York: Springer.

LeDoux, J. 1984. Sensory systems and emotion. *Integrative Psychiatry* (4), 237–243.

Lewis, H. 1990. *A Question of Values.* San Francisco: Harper.

Lilly, John. 1972. *The Center of the Cyclone.* New York: Julian Press.

Locke, S. 1986. *The Healer Within.* New York: New American Library.

Manning, G., K. Curtis, and S. McMillen. 1999. *Stress.* Duluth, Minn.: Whole Person Associates.

Manson, J. 1992. New heart attack theory for Type A's. *The Atlanta Journal/The Atlanta Constitution.* November 18, D1.

Manuck, S., and P. Saab. 1992. The influence of age, sex, and family on Type A and hostile attitudes and behavior. *Health Psychology* 11(5):317–323.

Maslach, C. and W. B. Schaufeli. 1993. Historical and conceptual development of burnout. In *Professional Burnout*, edited by C. Maslach, W. B. Schaufeli, and T. Merek. Bristol, Penn.: Taylor and Francis.

Maslow, A. H. 1971. *Farther Reaches of Human Nature*. New York: Viking.

Matheny, K. B., and P. Cupp. 1983. Control, desirability, and anticipation as moderating variables between life change and illness. *Journal of Human Stress*, June, 14–23.

Matheny, K. B., E. Hamarat, and C. A. Edge. 2000. Coping strategies for the most undesirable life events of older Americans. Unpublished manuscript.

McCarthy, C. J., A. E. Seraphine, K. B. Matheny, and W. L. Curlette. 2000. Factor analysis of the coping resources inventory scales for educational enhancement. *Measurement and Evaluation in Counseling and Development* 32:199–215.

McClelland, D. C. 1985. *Human Motivation*. Glenview, Ill: Scott Foresman.

McClelland, D. C., and J. B. Jemmot. 1980. Power motivation, stress, and physical illness. *Journal of Human Stress* 6:6–15.

Meisner, W. W. 1977. Family process and psychosomatic disease. In *Psychosomatic Medicine, Current trends and clinical applications*. edited by Z. J. Lipowski, D. Lippsitt, and P. Whybrow. New York: Oxford University Press.

Miller, M.A., and R. H. Rahe. 1997. Life changes scaling for the 1990s. *Journal of Psychosomatic Research* 43(3):279–292.

Mroczek, D. K., and C. M. Kolarz. 1998. The effect of age on positive and negative affect: A developmental perspective on happiness. *Journal of Personality and Social Psychology* 75(5):1333–1349.

Myers, D. G. 1993. *The Pursuit of Happiness*. New York: Avon.

Naranjo, C., and R. E. Ornstein. 1971. *On the Psychology of Meditation*. New York: Viking Press.

Nietzsche, F. 1954. Twilight of the idols. In *The Portable Nietzsche*, edited and translated by W. Kaufman. New York: Viking Press.

Norretranders, Tor. 1998. *The User Illusion*. New York: Viking Press.

Osler, W. 1910. *Aequanimitas, with Other Addresses to Medical Students, Nurses, and Practitioners of Medicine*. Philadelphia: P. Blakiston's and Sons.

Parducci, A. 1995. *Happiness, Pleasure, and Judgment*. Mahwah, N.J.: Erlbaum.

Pavlov, I. P. 1928. *Lectures on Conditioned Reflexes*, vol. 1. W. H. Gantt, trans. London: Lawrence and Wishart.

Pennebaker, J. W. 1997. *Opening Up: The Healing Power of Expressin Emotions*. New York: Guilford.

Rabkin, J. G., and E. L. Struening. 1976. Life events, stress, and illness. *Science* 19(4):1013–1020.

Rifkin, J. 1987. *Time Wars*. New York: Holt.

Rosenthal, R. 1966. *Experimenter Effects on Behavior Research*. New York: Appleton-Century-Crofts.

Ruskin, J. 1851. *The Stones of Venice*. New York: DaCapo.

Russell, P. 1992. *The White Hole in Time*. San Francisco: Harper.

Sapolsky, R. M. 1998. *Why Zebras Don't Get Ulcers*. New York: W. H. Freeman and Company.

Schmich, Mary. 1997. Advice, like youth, probably just wasted on the young. *Chicago Tribune*, June 1.

Schor, J. B. 1992. *The Overworked American*. New York: Basic Books.

———. 1998. *The Overspent American*. New York: Basic Books.

Schucman, H., and W. Thetford. 1976. *A Course in Miracles*. Mill Valley, Calif.: Foundation for Inner Peace.

Schwartz, B. 1994. *The Costs of Living*. New York: Norton.

Selye, H. 1956. *The Stress of Life*. New York: McGraw-Hill.

———. 1976. *The Stress of Life*, rev. ed. New York: McGraw-Hill.

Shapiro, A. L. 1999. *The Control Revolution*. New York: Century Foundation.

Siegel, B. S. 1986. *Love, Medicine and Miracles*. New York: Harper and Row.

Silver, M. H., E. Bubrick, E. Jilinskaia, and T. T. Perls. 1998. Is there a centenarian personality? Paper presented at the 106th Annual Convention of the American Psychological Association. San Francisco.

Simeons, A. T. W. 1961. *Man's Presumptuous Brain*. New York: E. P. Dutton.

Simonton, O. C., and S. Simonton. 1975. Belief systems and the management of the emotional aspects of malignancy. *Journal of Transpersonal Psychology* 7:29–47.

Smith, H. 1987. *The Religions of Man*. New York: Paragon House.

Snyder, Gary. 1990. *The Practice of the Wild*. New York: North Point Press.

Stevens, B. 1985. *Don't Push the River*. Berkeley: Celestial Arts Publishing.

Stress: The "type A" hypothesis. 1992. *Harvard Heart Letter*, January.

Stroebel, C. 1978. *The Quieting Response Training*. New York: BMA.

Suzuki, S. 1970. *Zen Mind, Beginner's Mind*. New York: Weatherhill.

Talbot, M. 2000. The placebo prescription. *New York Times Magazine*, January 9, 35–39.

Temoshock, L., and H. Dreher. 1992. *The Type C Connection*. New York: Random House.

Terkel, S. 1975. *Working*. New York: Avon.

Toynbee, A. 1972. *The Study of History*. Oxford: Oxford University Press.

USA Today. 1998. I don't want to grow up. March 10, p. 10.

Velton, E. A. 1968. A laboratory task for the induction of mood states. *Behavior Research and Therapy* 6:573–582.

Volz, J. 2000. Successful aging: The second 50. *Monitor on Psychology* 31(1):24–28.

Watson, D. 1990. On the dispositional nature of stress measures: Stable and non-specific influences on self-reported hassles. *Personality Inquiry* 1:34–37.

Watzlawick, P., C. E. Weakland, and R. Fisch. 1974. *Change*. New York: W. W. Norton.

Weiner, J. 1999. Can I live to be 125? *Time*, November 8: p. 74.

Wilber, K. 1996. *A Brief History of Everything*. Boston: Shambhala.

Williams, R. B., T. L. Haney, K. L. Lee, Y. H. Kong, J. A. Blumenthal, and R. E. Whalen. 1980. Type A behavior, hostility, and coronary atherosclerosis. *Psychosomatic Medicine* 42:539–549.

Wyatt, J. K. 2000. Circadian rhythm sleep disorders. *The Health Psychologist* 22(1):5–15.

Wyler, A. R., M. Masuda, and T. H. Holmes. 1971. Magnitude of life events and seriousness of illness. *Psychosomatic Medicine* 33:115–122.

Zuckerman, M., M. S. Buchsbaum, and D. L. Murphy. 1980. Sensation seeking and its biological correlates. *Psychological Bulletin* 88:187–214.

Kenneth Matheny, Ph.D., ABPP, is Regents Professor and Director of the Counseling Psychology Program at Georgia State University. He is a Diplomate with the American Board of Professional Psychology, holds Fellow status with both the Academy of Counseling Psychology and the American Association of Applied and Preventive Psychology, and is a member of the American Psychological Association, the Georgia Psychological Association, and the International Stress Management Association. He consults widely with corporations and government agencies in the United States and several other countries regarding organizational stress and worker resilience, and he collaborates on stress research with researchers in eight other countries.

His previous books are *Stress and Strategies for Lifestyle Management; Therapy American Style: Person Power through Self-Help; A Case for Adlerian Counseling: Theory, Techniques, and Research Evidence;* and *The Function of Counseling Theory.*

Photo by David Culp

Christopher J. McCarthy, Ph.D. is an Assistant Professor, Dept. of Educational Psychology, University of Texas at Austin. His Ph.D. is in Counseling Psychology and he is a faculty member in the Counselor Education and Counseling Psychology Training Programs at UT-Austin.

He is a member of the American Counseling Association, the Texas Counseling Association, the American Educational Research Association, and the American Psychological Association.

More New Harbinger Titles

DON'T LET YOUR MIND STUNT YOUR GROWTH

Stories, Fables, and Techniques That Will Change the Ways You Think
This inspiring companion helps you challenge the thoughts or feelings that prevent you from experiencing your life in all its glorious, moment-to-moment reality. *Item MIND $10.95*

ENERGY TAPPING

How to Rapidly Eliminate Anxiety, Depression, Cravings, and More Using Energy Psychology
Step-by-step instructions show you how to use this breakthrough new technique, which allows you to literally tap into your own energy system, balance it, and begin to live a life free of nagging emotional pain, self-sabotage, and unresolved issues. *Item ETAP $14.95*

DANCING NAKED

Breaking through the Emotional Limits That Keep You from the Job You Want
A psychologist who specializes in career counseling helps you strip away defenses, embrace the uncertainties of today's job market, pinpoint your goals, and use contacts and resources to manage your career with confidence and maximum effectiveness. *Item DNCE $14.95*

THE DAILY RELAXER

Presents the most effective and popular techniques for learning how to relax—simple, tension-relieving exercises that you can learn in five minutes and practice with positive results right away. *Item DALY Paperback, $12.95*

PRACTICAL DREAMING

Awakening the Power of Dreams in Your Life
Explains how dream language works, describes techniques to help you remember dreams and ask them for guidance, and explains how to interpret a dream's symbols and relate the dream to your waking life. *Item DRMG $12.95*

Call **toll-free 1-800-748-6273** to order. Have your Visa or Mastercard number ready. Or send a check for the titles you want to New Harbinger Publications, 5674 Shattuck Avenue, Oakland, CA 94609. Include $3.80 for the first book and 75¢ for each additional book to cover shipping and handling. (California residents please include appropriate sales tax.) Allow four to six weeks for delivery.

Prices subject to change without notice.

Some Other New Harbinger Self-Help Titles

Multiple Chemical Sensitivity: A Survival Guide, $16.95
Dancing Naked, $14.95
Why Are We Still Fighting, $15.95
From Sabotage to Success, $14.95
Parkinson's Disease and the Art of Moving, $15.95
A Survivor's Guide to Breast Cancer, $13.95
Men, Women, and Prostate Cancer, $15.95
Make Every Session Count: Getting the Most Out of Your Brief Therapy, $10.95
Virtual Addiction, $12.95
After the Breakup, $13.95
Why Can't I Be the Parent I Want to Be?, $12.95
The Secret Message of Shame, $13.95
The OCD Workbook, $18.95
Tapping Your Inner Strength, $13.95
Binge No More, $14.95
When to Forgive, $12.95
Practical Dreaming, $12.95
Healthy Baby, Toxic World, $15.95
Making Hope Happen, $14.95
I'll Take Care of You, $12.95
Survivor Guilt, $14.95
Children Changed by Trauma, $13.95
Understanding Your Child's Sexual Behavior, $12.95
The Self-Esteem Companion, $10.95
The Gay and Lesbian Self-Esteem Book, $13.95
Making the Big Move, $13.95
How to Survive and Thrive in an Empty Nest, $13.95
Living Well with a Hidden Disability, $15.95
Overcoming Repetitive Motion Injuries the Rossiter Way, $15.95
What to Tell the Kids About Your Divorce, $13.95
The Divorce Book, Second Edition, $15.95
Claiming Your Creative Self: True Stories from the Everyday Lives of Women, $15.95
Six Keys to Creating the Life You Desire, $19.95
Taking Control of TMJ, $13.95
What You Need to Know About Alzheimer's, $15.95
Winning Against Relapse: A Workbook of Action Plans for Recurring Health and Emotional Problems, $14.95
Facing 30: Women Talk About Constructing a Real Life and Other Scary Rites of Passage, $12.95
The Worry Control Workbook, $15.95
Wanting What You Have: A Self-Discovery Workbook, $18.95
When Perfect Isn't Good Enough: Strategies for Coping with Perfectionism, $13.95
Earning Your Own Respect: A Handbook of Personal Responsibility, $12.95
High on Stress: A Woman's Guide to Optimizing the Stress in Her Life, $13.95
Infidelity: A Survival Guide, $13.95
Stop Walking on Eggshells, $14.95
Consumer's Guide to Psychiatric Drugs, $16.95
The Fibromyalgia Advocate: Getting the Support You Need to Cope with Fibromyalgia and Myofascial Pain, $18.95
Healing Fear: New Approaches to Overcoming Anxiety, $16.95
Working Anger: Preventing and Resolving Conflict on the Job, $12.95
Sex Smart: How Your Childhood Shaped Your Sexual Life and What to Do About It, $14.95
You Can Free Yourself From Alcohol & Drugs, $13.95
Amongst Ourselves: A Self-Help Guide to Living with Dissociative Identity Disorder, $14.95
Healthy Living with Diabetes, $13.95
Dr. Carl Robinson's Basic Baby Care, $10.95
Better Boundaries: Owning and Treasuring Your Life, $13.95
Goodbye Good Girl, $12.95
Fibromyalgia & Chronic Myofascial Pain Syndrome, $19.95
The Depression Workbook: Living With Depression and Manic Depression, $17.95
Self-Esteem, Second Edition, $13.95
Angry All the Time: An Emergency Guide to Anger Control, $12.95
When Anger Hurts, $13.95
Perimenopause, $16.95
The Relaxation & Stress Reduction Workbook, Fourth Edition, $17.95
The Anxiety & Phobia Workbook, Second Edition, $18.95
I Can't Get Over It, A Handbook for Trauma Survivors, Second Edition, $16.95
Messages: The Communication Skills Workbook, Second Edition, $15.95
Thoughts & Feelings, Second Edition, $18.95
Depression: How It Happens, How It's Healed, $14.95
The Deadly Diet, Second Edition, $14.95
The Power of Two, $15.95

Call **toll free, 1-800-748-6273**, or log on to our online bookstore at **www.newharbinger.com** to order. Have your Visa or Mastercard number ready. Or send a check for the titles you want to New Harbinger Publications, Inc., 5674 Shattuck Ave., Oakland, CA 94609. Include $3.80 for the first book and 75¢ for each additional book, to cover shipping and handling. (California residents please include appropriate sales tax.) Allow two to five weeks for delivery.

Prices subject to change without notice.